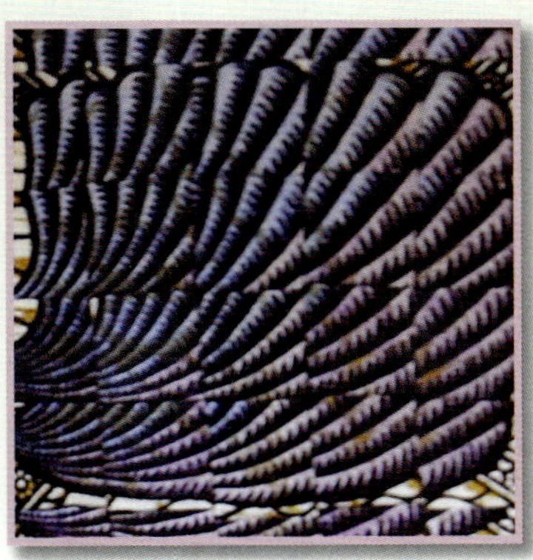

Shatter and Sew!

Introducing the Shattered Image™ Technique

by Connie Mantini

Edited by Patricia Faust

Published by

WRITE DIMENSIONS

NOTE: Fabrics used in the projects shown might not be currently available since fabric manufacturers keep most fabrics in print for only a short time.

Edited by: Patricia Faust
Book layout: Dawn Andone, Patricia Faust, Connie Mantini
Graphic consultant: Digital Mirrors
Printed by: A Carlisle & Company of Reno, Nevada

Library of Congress Cataloging-in-Publication Data

Mantini, Connie.
Shatter and Sew, 1st edition, c2009
p.cm
ISBN-978-0-615-23600-1 (pbk.)

Library of Congress Control Number: 2008934449

GETTING STARTED

CHAPTER 1

THE BASICS

CHAPTER 2

IDEAS GALLERY

CHAPTER 3

BEYOND BASICS

CHAPTER 4

ELLEN'S GALLERY

CHAPTER 5

Acknowledgements

To the many who helped me make this book a reality:

Peter Harris
Ellen's partner who shared information about Ellen, photos of her projects, and encouraged the writing of this book.

Corinne Baumbach
for bringing the technique to life for me.

Linda Bracco
for sharing the "Pick Up the Squares" technique.

Leslie Sei and Juanita Tower
for testing the book instructions and offering wonderful suggestions.

Dave Mantini
for his help as a photographer and his encouragement in moving the manuscript to completion.

Dawn Andone
for her help in designing the layout of the book and her invaluable review comments.

and contributions from
**Lisa Eldridge, Karen Kilgore, Ann Kuehl,
Mary Mantini, Carol Stephen, and Paula Walkins**

Special thanks to
Patricia Faust
*for her help in designing the layout of the book, identifying usability issues, and editing.
But most of all, for being a friend who has been at my side throughout this project.*

Ellen Adams created the Shattered Image technique presented in this book.

Ellen was an award-winning fiber artist and quilter. Her intricate patterns suggest motion and dynamic energy, inviting us to see the world as a "fragmented array of vibrant color."

Ellen was born in Toronto, Canada in 1941. She attended the University of British Columbia, earning a Bachelor of Science (with honors) in 1962 and a Master of Arts in 1964, both degrees in zoology. She started out as an associate in biochemistry research at Brandeis University in Massachusetts, and then worked for several years as a film editor in London, England.

In 1971, Ellen returned to Canada as a freelance feature film sound editor, which took her ultimately to the centers of the film industry, New York and Los Angeles. During her spare time, she photographed Art Deco building interiors and exteriors. And then she found quilting!

In 1979, Ellen designed and made a quilt inspired by Art Deco doors she had photographed. The quilt was very large – the size of the doors! She used silks, satins, and velvets and made it simply because she "wanted one to sleep under."

Back in Canada, Ellen studied design at the Ontario College of Art in Toronto. She graduated (with honors) in 1985, and, with her partner Peter Harris, a tapestry weaver, ventured to India to informally study textiles. Later she taught for several years at the fabrics studio at Sheridan College in Oakville, Canada.

Ellen's article sharing her Shattered Image technique was published in *Threads* magazine in 1999. That article was the inspiration for this book and for many fun and exciting creative projects. Chapter 5 in this book shows Ellen's Shattered Image projects.

Ellen succumbed to colon cancer in July 2001. The world lost an incredible artist, teacher, and quilter.

Photograph by Peter Harris
circa 1990

CHAPTER 1

Getting Started

Welcome

The first Shattered Image project I saw was a wall hanging in a quilt store made using a Japanese floral. I stared at that wall hanging like it was modern art in a museum and wondered, how do you do that? I couldn't figure it out and I did not find books on the technique — I did find a class. I assumed the technique had to be complicated to create such dynamic results – was I ever wrong! The concept is so simple!

The Shattered Image technique is a fast, easy way to cut each repeat *separately* into squares and then arrange each square on a grid. The minimum number of image repeats used is 4; the maximum can be any number. This book describes how to use 4, 9, and 16-repeats. To make a 4-repeat project, you need 4 repeats of an image; a 9-repeat requires 9 and so on.

But what other motifs could work besides flowers? Flowers look wonderful with just about every technique. Well I used cars, fruit, animals, and geometric designs and for a couple of motifs, I made all repeat versions (4, 9, and 16) just to see the differences.

I discovered that this technique can be used in all kinds of projects. That's when I realized that I wanted to share my work with you – my results are throughout this book. In it, you see how to create the Shattered Image illusion, using step-by-step directions so that you won't have to go through the trial-by-error method, like I did. It includes a variety of project samples using the different motifs so you can see what works and doesn't work for you and it helps preserve a wonderful technique!

So, let's get shattering!

Connie

Ellen Adams created a fast and easy way to cut images into squares and reassemble them so cleverly that floral images appear to bloom, images of animals or vehicles seem to move, and shapes diffuse to abstraction.

Getting the Most from This Book

This book is organized to get you shattering from the simplest project to the more complex. I suggest you begin with…

Chapters

1. Getting Started — Prepare for making a 4, 9, or 16-repeat shattered project by learning how to select fabric, choose your focal point, decide on a square size, make a template, and cut your repeats.

2. The Basics — Start with the simplest Shattered Image technique, commonly called the 4-repeat. Follow the clearly illustrated steps.

3. Ideas Gallery — Visit the gallery to see projects that students and friends have made as inspiration for your own Shattered Image project.

4. Beyond Basics — Learn the more complex 9 and 16-repeat versions of this technique.

5. Ellen's Gallery — Admire Ellen's collection of Shattered Image work and read her comments and suggestions! Ellen used 9 and 16-repeats in her projects.

Worksheets — Copy and use the worksheets on pages 83 and 84 to practice with paper and save your fabric! If you choose this *jump in and do it* approach, go directly to Chapter 2.

Shattered Notes — Read the tips and comments that tell you what works or doesn't work, how to save money and time, and what to be aware of!

Blooms on Blue

Original size: 8 x 10 inches

Shattered size: 11 x 14½ inches

Finished computer screen cover size: 16½ x 21 inches

2-inch squares

Supply List

Although this book shows samples made using fabric,
you can use other materials such as paper or photographs.

Required

Fabric

Projects in this book are made primarily with 100% cotton.
Some projects use a number of other fabrics and blends, such as
50% cotton and 50% polyester, 100% polyester, 100% rayon and
washable wool, satin, and velvet.

Template Plastic

1 medium-sized sheet, or a sheet larger than your image. **(See 1)**

Fabric Marker

Such as Vanishing Fabric Marker, Chaco-Liner, or pencils
that wash out. **(2)**

Grid Fabric

1 yard or more of grid fabric, depending on your project size. You
can use Pellon Quilter's Grid™, Maywood Creative Grid (Universal
Design Grid) **(3)**, Blockbutler® design wall, or a flannel board.

Quilter's Ruler

6 x 24 inches or 3 x 18 inches **(4)**

Rotary Cutter

See **(5)**

Cutting Mat

See **(6)**

Required

Picture Frame   Or use a frame mat, poster or cardboard, or strips of paper to isolate your focal point.

Scissors   Or use an old rotary blade to cut the template plastic.

Marking Pencil   Or use other nonpermanent marker to mark your template.

Masking Tape   Use to mark directional arrows on the top row of squares.

Looking at the Garden in the Rain

Original size: 14 x 16 inches

Shattered size:
18½ x 21¾ inches

Finished wall hanging size:
26 x 29 inches

2-inch squares

Optional

Pins   Use straight or safety pins to secure the squares to the grid.

Ruler   Shape Cut™ Plus, quilt tool by June Taylor, to cut your squares faster.

Spray Starch   Or use sizing to give body to light-weight fabrics.

Steam-a-Seam®   Use to iron squares to a fabric instead of sewing.

1. Choose Fabric

Your fabric choice depends on what effect you want to achieve! Here are a few **guidelines** for selecting fabric for this technique.

What Fabric Works?

Generally, when choosing fabric:

- Choose a **specific** image—like a flower.

- Choose an **area** if your fabric is abstract or has a continuous design.

The **key** is to find a focal point or area of the fabric. Here are some examples of motifs that work. Each identifies a specific reason why the fabric works for this technique.

Different-sized images with distinct colors.

Some border prints. This floral sample is used throughout Chapters 2 and 4.

Images that are at least 3 inches by 3 inches.

Fabric with backgrounds, such as marbling, swirls, or plaid can work. See Carol Juillerat's sample on page 34.

Space or eye rest around the individual images.

What Doesn't Work

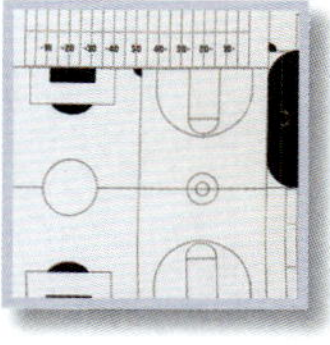

Fabric with lines.

A diffused pattern.

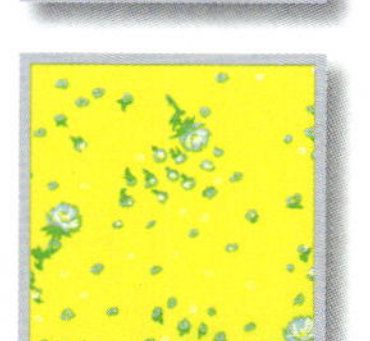

Small motif, large background.

Save these types of fabric designs for another project, because the lines, diffused pattern, or small motif show little to no movement and lose definition. Fabric designs with large backgrounds will dwarf the small motif.

Next, let's talk about *Pre-Printed Panels.*

I use the 4-repeat as an example, but all information in this chapter is the same for 9 or 16-repeat versions.

Pre-Printed Panels

Be aware of pre-printed panels with borders. Look at the borders around the original panels of the parrots, on the right.

Now, look below and compare the shattered borders in both *Pair of Parrots* and *Blue Bouncer*. The *Pair of Parrots* border is jagged.

Pair of Parrots

Blue Bouncer

Look at the leopards in *Shivering Spots* below. The original panel had a border, which I removed and then used to reframe the shattered lap quilt.

So, if you use fabric with a border, consider it carefully when cutting and sewing your squares or remove it before shattering. It is easier to remove the border and use it later than to shatter the border.

Shivering Spots

Original panel size: 16 x 16 inches

Shattered panel size: 21¾ x 21¾ inches

2-inch squares

Original panel size: 21 x 30 inches (without the frame)

Shattered panel size: 36½ x 48 inches

4-inch squares

Stained-Glass Poinsettia

Original size: 9 x 30 inches

Shattered size: 11¾ x 36½ inches

Finished table runner size:
15 x 40 inches

3-inch squares, batik

So, How Much Fabric Do You Need?

You need enough fabric to cut the required number of identical image repeats.

While you only need 4 repeats to produce the basic Shattered Image project, it's really great if you have an extra image to put on the back of your finished project.

All projects are different, so the amount of fabric you need depends on…

- The size of the image you choose

- The number of repeats (4, 9, or 16)

- If you cut your repeats lengthwise or across the fabric

So, for the 4-repeat, *Stained-Glass Poinsettia* table runner shown here, I cut repeats across the fabric, 5 original images (placing 1 original on the back), using 3 yards. You can use image repeats across the fabric, but the repeats are not as precise.

Do You Like Precision?

If you want to be very precise, cut all your images from the lengthwise repeats of the fabric. You can tell the length of the repeat by looking at the selvedge for the registration marks, which show little dots of color, the fabric maker, and the designer. Each registration mark down the length of the fabric shows the single design that is repeated as the printer drum rolls over the fabric.

If a particular motif (say a flower) appears multiple times across the width of the fabric, it might look the same to your eye, but it might not actually be identical. Slight distortions can happen with fabric during printing and finishing.

But the same flower appearing in multiple repeats down the length of the fabric is identical to all others, because it was printed by exactly the same design on the drum.

Hand-printed fabrics, such as batiks, pose a special challenge because the designs are not as consistent as those on commercial fabrics.

So it may be best, when you are using hand-printed fabrics, to use the repeats lengthwise on the fabric.

2. Choose an Image or a Focal Point

Choosing a focal point is important because it affects all other steps in the process, as well as the appearance of the finished project. To find your focal point:

1. Spread out your fabric.
2. Put a picture frame or mat on the fabric, and move it around to help you isolate an area.
3. Are the copies of the image you like too close together? Then…
   - Continue moving your frame around until you find an image you can cut without interfering with other repeats of that image.
   - Change the size of the frame to fit your image so it does not overlap other repeats.
4. Once you find the image, can you divide the length and width evenly by 2, 3, or 4? In this example, my frame shows an 8 x 10-inch focal point—both 8 and 10 can be divided evenly by 2.

Why is that important? Fractions! Fractions can add complexity when you decide on a square size.

Let's talk square size next!

Shattered Note

Don't Limit Yourself!

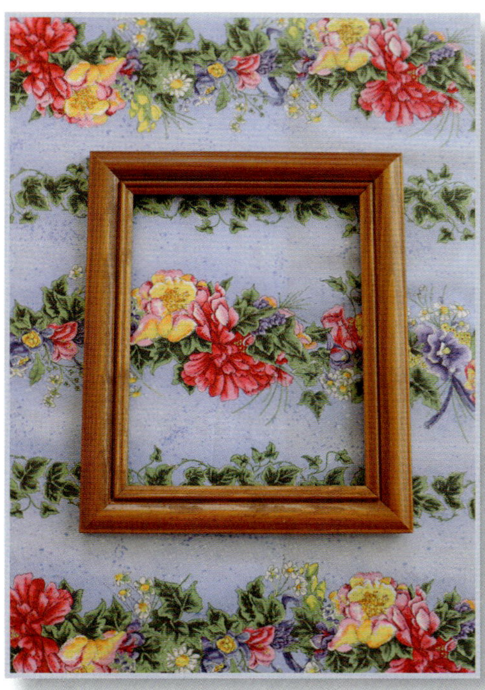

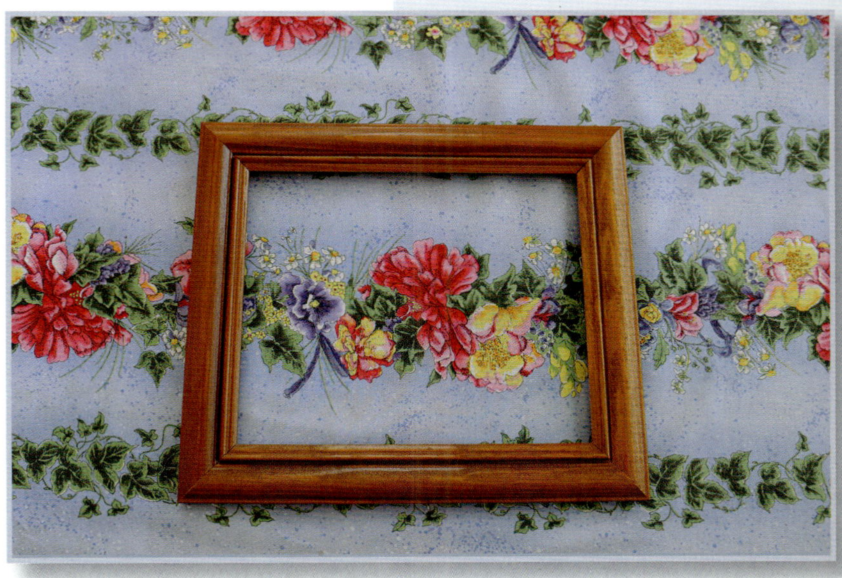

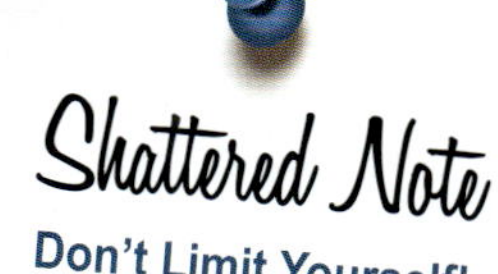

If you buy fabric for a specific image that seems wonderful for the Shattered Image technique, always take time to explore more. One student bought sea-animal fabric for one whale view. However, when we moved the frame around the fabric, we found a more interesting whale image with more colors and plants. The completed project had more movement and color. It was stunning!

See ***Playing Coy*** by Juanita Tower on page 39. She found 4 approaches using koi-fish fabric.

Image size: 8 x 10 inches

If you are using your fabric, take some time to consider the best square size for your image.

3. Decide on a Square Size

Once you have chosen your fabric and focal point, then decide on an appropriate square size for the size of your image.

So, how does square size relate to the image you choose? In general, if the square size for your image is too…

- **Small**
  you see less illusion of movement or expansion

- **Large**
  you see a ragged and disjointed image

Your choice of square size depends on the size of your original image and on the design elements within the image. Using an original 8 x 10-inch image, see how the square size changes with 1, 2, 3, and 4-inch squares.

I don't like fractions. So, looking at the size of my focal point and my 8 x 10 image, the 2-inch square looks the best! Also, 2 divides evenly into 8 and 10.

However, depending on the size of your image and the illusion you want to achieve, you can cut squares of any size from 1 to 6 inches and in fractional dimensions, if needed.

1-inch squares
barely expand the focal point

2-inch squares
the flowers begin to bloom

3-inch squares
the flowers expand further

4-inch squares
the expansion loses definition

The Effects of Square Size

Let's look at some examples to see how the size of the square can make a difference.

The original image of Harry Potter was a pre-printed panel. It was cut down slightly to measure 25 x 35 inches, so a 5-inch square seemed appropriate. Look how the light from Harry's wand really sweeps. It's quite dramatic!

But Harry's face looks a bit jagged and multiplied. In this case, there is a big difference between the smallest design element (Harry's face) and the largest (the sweep of light from the wand).

This is a good illustration of how even though the overall image is quite large, it may contain a smaller (and important) design element. I think this Shattered Image might have looked nicer using 3 or 4-inch squares because of the facial elements. So, people's faces might not always shatter well.

Fish Story
by Karen Kilgore

Now, look at these fish! The original fish are 5½ inches long and 1½ inches tall. This is cut with a 3-inch square. As you can see, the 3-inch square shattered the length of the fish just fine, but the 3-inch square size is a bit large for the height of the fish. So, animal prints can have a good or not-so-good end result.

Just look at Ellen's **Sixteen Cats and Nine Fleas** *or* **Self Portrait** *in Chapter 5 to see how animal and face prints can work.*

Size of Square	Cut your template into a size divisible by…
2 inches	2, such as: 8 x 8, 6 x 10, 12 x 16, and so on.
3 inches	3, such as: 6 x 9, 12 x 18, and so on.
4 inches	4, such as 12 x 16, 16 x 20, and so on.

4. Make a Template

The plastic template helps you cut identical fabric repeats. So, you can measure and cut the template once you decide on…

- The size of your image
  (in my example it is 8 x 10 inches)

- Your square size
  (in my example it is 2-inch squares)

On your fabric, does your image size divide evenly by your square size? In my example, 8 and 10 divide by 2 evenly.

- If you need to go back to change your template size to avoid fractions, do so now.

- If you changed your template size, does the whole image still work?

- If it does not work, you may need to search for another image or change your square size.

Measure and Cut the Template

1. Using a black pen and ruler, **measure** the plastic template. Begin at a corner of the plastic so you have enough template plastic left over for other projects.

2. Using scissors or an old rotary blade, **cut** the template. (Cutting plastic can dull a rotary blade, so use an old one.)

A template includes a seam allowance of up to ¼ inch.

5. Outline and Cut the Repeats

At this point, you are now ready to place your template on your fabric and cut the repeats.

Trace Three Areas

1. Place your template over the fabric focal point. Make sure you…
   - Do not have a selvedge in the image.

     Selvedges can pull and shrink differently from the rest of the fabric, which can distort your final product.
   - Have at least ¾ inch around the image.
   - Have enough identical images to do a 4, 9, or 16-repeat.
2. With an erasable pen, trace at least **3 separate areas of the design** on the template. Use these marks to accurately position your template over each of your other image repeats when you outline them. Use an erasable marker, so you can clean and reuse the template later.

Shattered Note

Don't Cut Yourself Short!

The ***Horse-Around*** bag shows the importance of at least a ¾-inch allowance around the original image. The horses on the top had ¾ inch around the image, so those horses kept their heads. But the horses shown at the bottom did not have the ¾ inch around the image because I did not have enough fabric. With a ¼-inch seam allowance, part of the head was cut off. Look at these poor horses and weep!

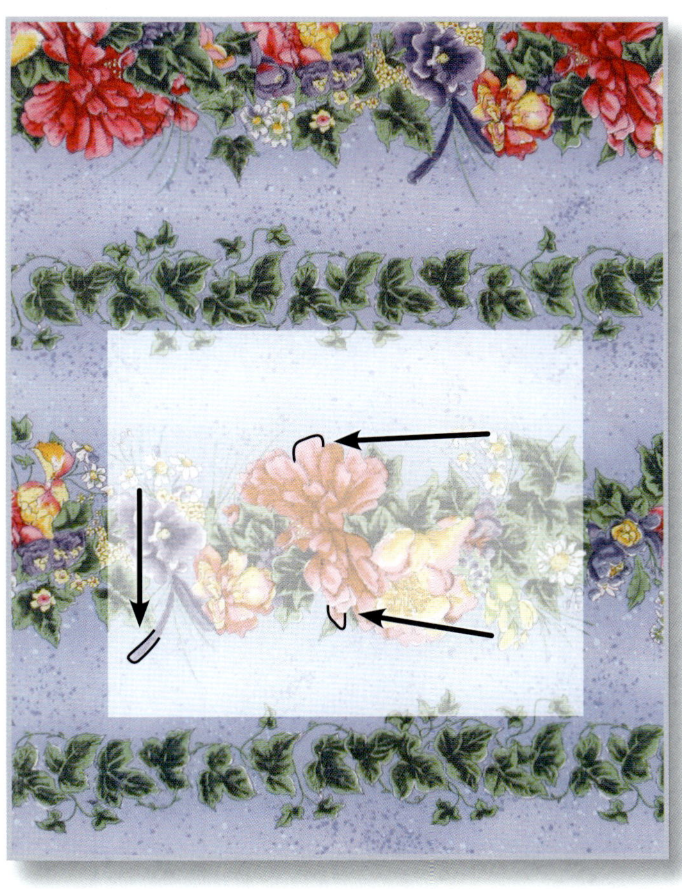

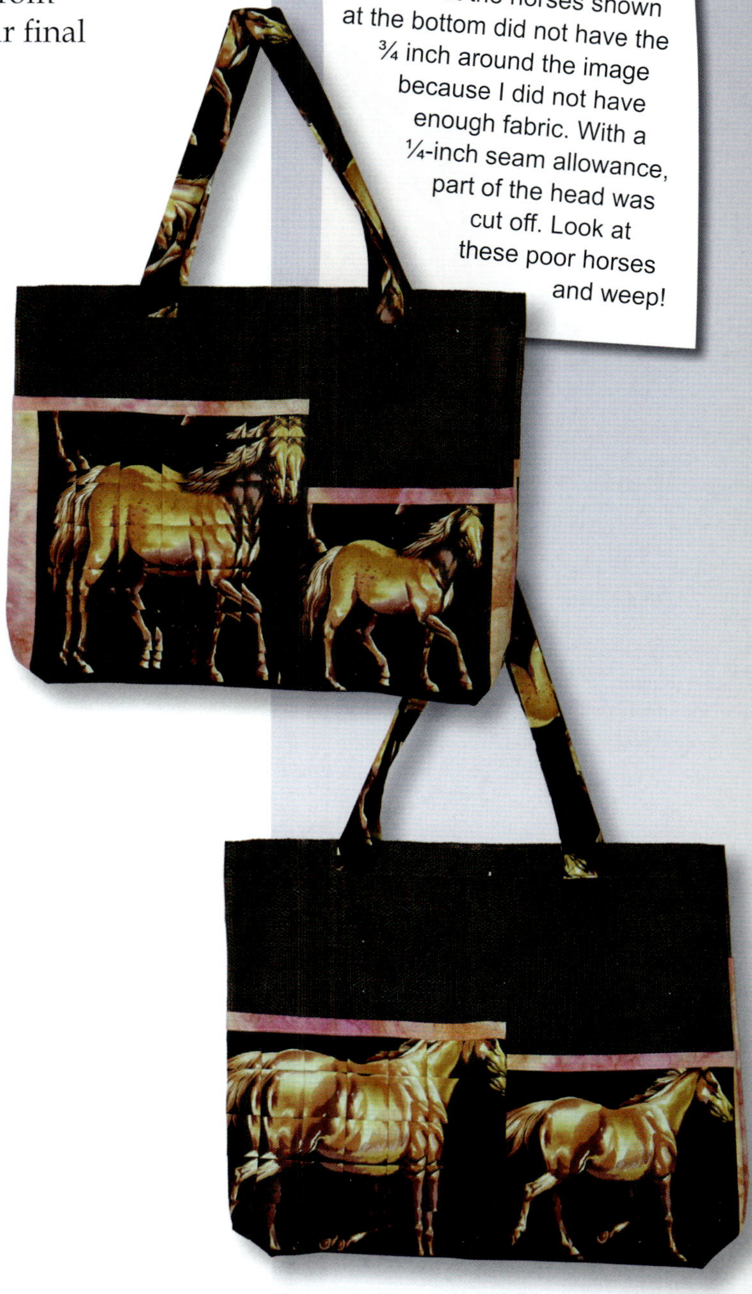

Cut an extra repeat if you want to put an original on the back of your project.

Outline the Template

You can outline the template with a pen, but, to be safe, use something washable. Sometimes a pen accidentally leaks or catches on the fabric and skips outside the intended area, making your fabric unusable. However, you may like a fabric pencil because it can be kept sharp, and it makes a fine, precise line.

1. Position and outline the template. I use Chaco-Liner to draw around the template.

2. At the top left of the template, write the…

    - Image size, for example, 8 x 10 inches

    - Square size, 2 inches

In the future, if you want to make a shattered project the same size, just look for that size template.

Cut the Repeats

3. Cut your image repeats.

4. Orient the repeats so they all face the same direction. Here you see the pansy is on the left.

5. Set aside one image repeat to put on the back of your finished project.

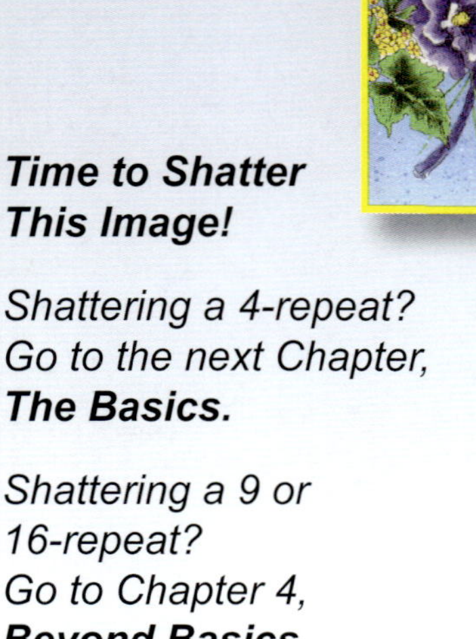

Time to Shatter This Image!

Shattering a 4-repeat? Go to the next Chapter, **The Basics.**

Shattering a 9 or 16-repeat? Go to Chapter 4, **Beyond Basics.**

Count Before Cutting

I made my brother a shirt from this hot-rod fabric. Since I had scraps left over, I thought it would be interesting to see how this hot-rod motif would look shattered.

I found a focal point and counted 4 repeats. But my eyes tricked me. When I began outlining each repeat with chalk, I found I only had 3 repeats. I had 2 choices – cut another repeat from my brother's shirt or find a new focal point. Well, because I outlined my repeats with chalk before cutting them, my brother didn't lose his shirt. I found another focal point, which you see here.

Hot Rod in Motion

Original size:
8 x 8 inches

Shattered size:
10½ x 10½ inches

Finished pillow size:
14 x 14 inches

2-inch squares

CHAPTER 2

The Basics

4-Repeat

The 4-repeat is the simplest form of the Shattered Image technique. You need at least 4 copies of the worksheets or 4 repeats of your fabric to produce this shattered effect. For this version, you will be cutting the 4 repeats into 1 Anchor and 3 Offsets. Each repeat is cut *separately* into squares, and then each square is arranged on a grid.

This chapter takes you through the steps to cut, arrange, and sew the squares to create a Shattered Image. Then, I've included directions for making a placemat to finish the project.

Each letter (A, B, C, D) represents a repeat.

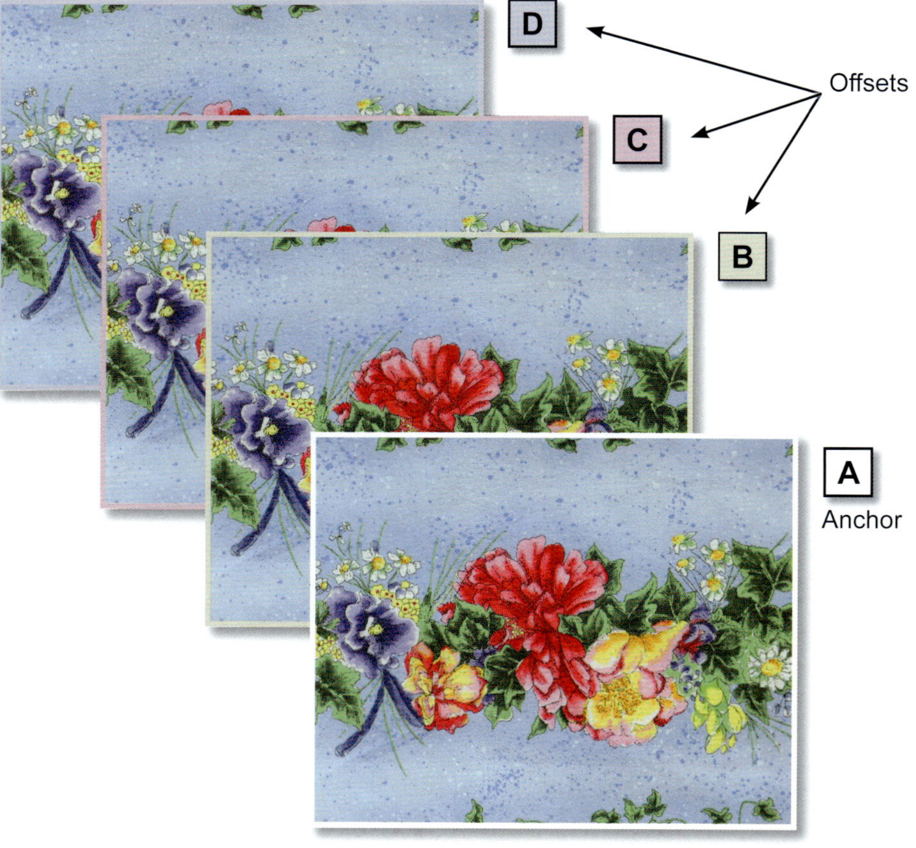

Anchor and Offset Squares

Anchor Squares – Squares cut from the first image repeat are the Anchor squares (labeled **A**). These squares are the foundation from which you expand the image.

Offset Squares – The remaining image repeats (labeled **B**, **C**, and **D**) surround each Anchor square. Together, they expand your original image into a Shattered Image.

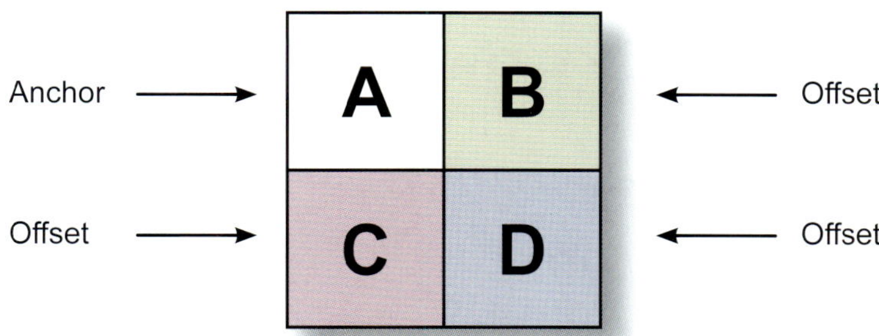

Grid-to-Repeat Relationship

The grid helps you place your squares to create the Shattered Image pattern. I have added numbers to each grid square to help identify the exact placement of each Anchor and Offset square on the grid.

When you begin arranging the squares on the grid…you begin to see the shattered effect. It is also the first place you can detect if you misplaced a square in the arrangement. This is good because you can readjust the misplaced square before sewing!

You do not need to mark your grid!

A1	B1	A2	B2	A3
C1	D1	C2	D2	C3
A4	B3	A5	B4	A6

Repeat A – Cut and Arrange Squares

Let's get started!

1. Spread out your **grid** fabric on a separate work area (not your cutting mat).

2. Orient your 4 repeats in the same direction.

3. Take 1 repeat and put it on your cutting mat. You will be cutting this repeat into the Anchor squares.

4. Using a marking pencil, measure and tic-mark 2-inch increments around the image, beginning at the top-left corner of the image repeat. (Skip this step if you are using a **quilter's ruler** or the June Taylor Shape Cut™ guide.)

5. Cut the repeats into **squares**.

   - Cut the **columns**. Use a rotary cutter and quilter's ruler to cut this repeat into 2-inch columns—be sure the cut columns stay fixed in position before cutting the rows. (If you are not using a quilter's ruler, use a ruler to match the tic-marks on top and bottom to cut the columns and side to side to cut the rows.)

   - Cut the **rows**. With the columns cut, follow the same procedure to cut the rows.
   Don't move anything!

Add Directional Markers

1. Cut 5 pieces of masking tape.

2. Draw an arrow on each piece, and put the tape only on the **top** row of squares to indicate the direction of your image.

You don't need to number your squares. Just add the tape to the top rows.

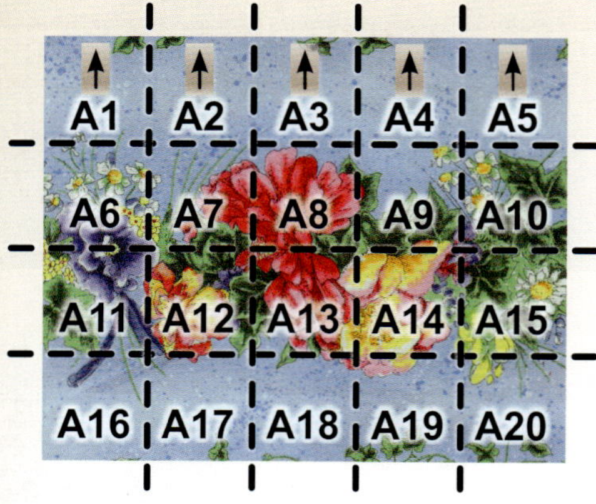

Top Row—Pick Up the Squares

1. Pick up the **top-left square** from your cutting mat.

2. Moving across the row from left to right, pick up and put each square directly **under** the square you are holding.

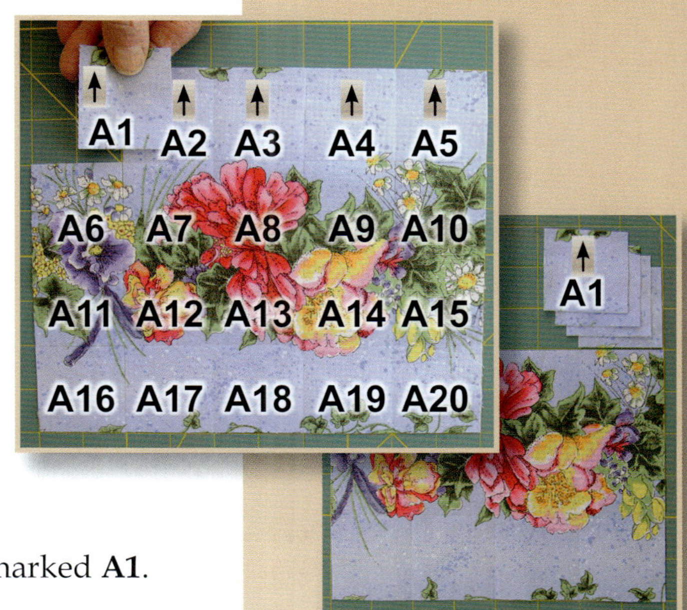

Top Row—Place the Squares

Below you see the grid squares marked to show you where to put each Anchor square.

1. Place the top square you are holding in the grid marked **A1**.

2. Skip the next grid block and place the next square in **A2**.

3. Skip the next block and place the next square in **A3**, and so on until you have placed your top row of squares.

Second Row—Pick Up the Squares

1. Beginning at the first square in the next row, pick up the **left** square (**A6**).

2. Moving across the row to the right (**A7** - **A10**), pick up and put each square directly **under** the **A6** square.

Second Row—Place the Squares

1. Skip the grid row under squares A1 - A5.

2. Place the **A6** square as shown in the third grid row.

3. Skip the next grid block and place the next square in **A7**.

4. Skip the next block and place the next in **A8**, and so on until you have placed your second row of squares.

5. Now, follow the same process of picking up and arranging the last two Anchor (A) rows.

You are now ready to cut the next image repeat.

A1		A2		A3		A4		A5
A6		A7		A8		A9		A10
A11		A12		A13		A14		A15
A16		A17		A18		A19		A20

Repeat B – Cut and Arrange Squares

Repeat B is the first repeat you are cutting into Offset squares.

1. Put another image repeat on the cutting mat. Make sure this image is oriented in the same direction as repeat A.

2. Measure and trim 1 inch only from the **sides** of this image.

3. Cut the newly trimmed image into 2-inch squares.

   - Cut **columns** as you did for repeat A.

   - Cut **rows** as you did for repeat A.

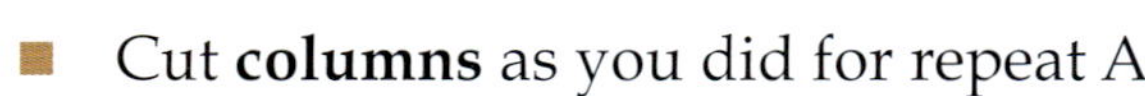

Add Directional Markers

4. Cut pieces of masking tape and draw an **arrow** on each piece.

5. Place the pieces of tape with an arrow on the **top** row to identify the direction of your image, as you did for repeat **A**.

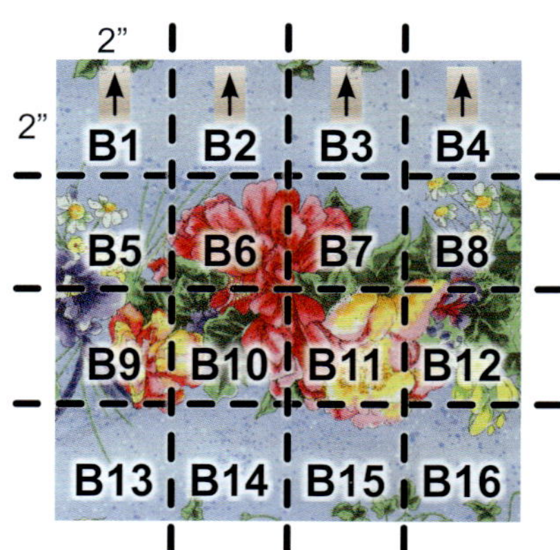

Pick Up the Squares

6. Beginning at the top-left corner of your image, pick up the squares in the same way as you did for repeat A.

Place the Squares

1. Looking at the top row of your **grid** fabric, place the top square in the **B1** grid.

2. Skip the A2 grid block and place the next square in **B2**.

3. Skip the A3 block and place the next square in **B3**, and so on until you have placed the top row of your squares.

4. Pick up the remaining rows of squares and place them as shown in the diagram in the **B**-designated spaces.

A1	**B1**	A2	**B2**	A3	**B3**	A4	**B4**	A5
A6	**B5**	A7	**B6**	A8	**B7**	A9	**B8**	A10
A11	**B9**	A12	**B10**	A13	**B11**	A14	**B12**	A15
A16	**B13**	A17	**B14**	A18	**B15**	A19	**B16**	A20

Shattered Note

Too Much Help!

If you have small children or a helpful dog or cat, secure each square to the grid-fabric with a straight or safety pin to make sure the square does not take flight and you lose time trying to rearrange or start over.

You can pin each square as you place it on the grid. Here, all the Dinos are pinned to a Pellon 1-inch Quilter's Grid.

Repeat C – Cut and Arrange Squares

1. Put another image repeat on the cutting mat. Make sure this image is oriented in the same direction as the previous repeats.

2. Measure and trim 1 inch only from the **top** and **bottom** of this image.

3. Cut the trimmed image into 2-inch squares.

   ■ Cut **columns** as you did for repeat A.

   ■ Cut **rows** as you did for repeat A.

Only the top row (A and B squares) needs directional arrows.

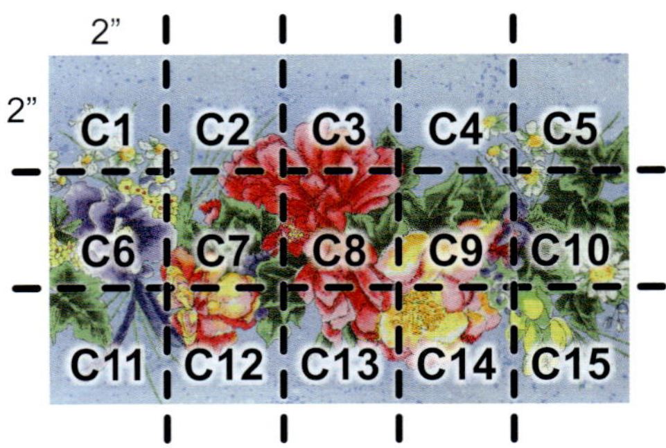

Pick Up and Place the Squares

4. Beginning at the top-left corner, pick up the top row of **C** squares as you did for the previous repeats.

5. Place those squares in the **C**-designated spaces.

6. Pick up the remaining rows of squares and place them in the **C**-designated spaces.

A1	B1	A2	B2	A3	B3	A4	B4	A5
C1		C2		C3		C4		C5
A6	B5	A7	B6	A8	B7	A9	B8	A10
C6		C7		C8		C9		C10
A11	B9	A12	B10	A13	B11	A14	B12	A15
C11		C12		C13		C14		C15
A16	B13	A17	B14	A18	B15	A19	B16	A20

Repeat D – Cut and Arrange Squares

1. Put another image repeat on the cutting mat. Make sure this image is oriented in the same direction as the previous repeats.

2. Measure and trim 1 inch from…

   - The **top** and **bottom**
   - **Both sides**

3. Cut the trimmed image into 2-inch squares as before.

Pick Up and Place the Squares

4. Pick up the top row of **D** squares as you did for the previous repeats.

5. Place those squares in the **D**-designated spaces.

6. Pick up the remaining rows of squares and place them in the **D**-designated spaces.

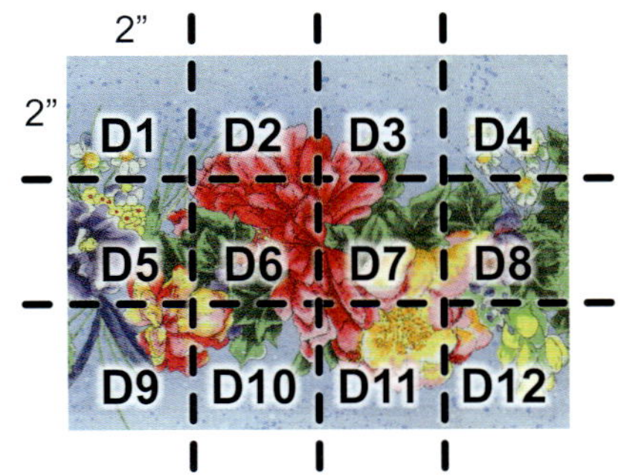

4-Repeat Final Layout

The diagram shows a complete layout of all squares for a 4-repeat Shattered Image.

Check to see that the squares are not turned or out of place, so that your image expands properly.

A1	B1	A2	B2	A3	B3	A4	B4	A5
C1	**D1**	C2	**D2**	C3	**D3**	C4	**D4**	C5
A6	B5	A7	B6	A8	B7	A9	B8	A10
C6	**D5**	C7	**D6**	C8	**D7**	C9	**D8**	C10
A11	B9	A12	B10	A13	B11	A14	B12	A15
C11	**D9**	C12	**D10**	C13	**D11**	C14	**D12**	C15
A16	B13	A17	B14	A18	B15	A19	B16	A20

Sew It Together

You are now ready to assemble your project. But first, you need to pick up your squares without turning or changing their sequence. Well, everyone may have their own way to pick up squares, but I want to share a way that is quick and easy! Begin by flipping the squares.

Flip the Squares

The easiest way to sew the squares together and keep them in the correct place is to flip, stack, and then sew.

Begin with the **two columns** on the left of your Shattered Image project.

1. Pick up the top square in column 2.

2. Put it right-side down on top of the column 1 top square. Make sure it faces in the same direction.

3. Continue to flip the rest of column 2 on top of column 1.

Stack the Squares

The first column is now 2 squares deep.

1. Beginning with the **top-left flipped squares**, pick up those squares and move down the column to the next square.

2. Put the stack on **top** of the squares in the column. Pick up the stack. You are now holding 4 squares.

3. Move down the column and put the stack you are holding on **top** of the next flipped set of squares in the column. Pick up the stack.

4. Move down the column, pick up the stack, and put it on **top** of the next set of squares.

5. Continue moving down the first column. You now have one stack of squares from the 2 columns.

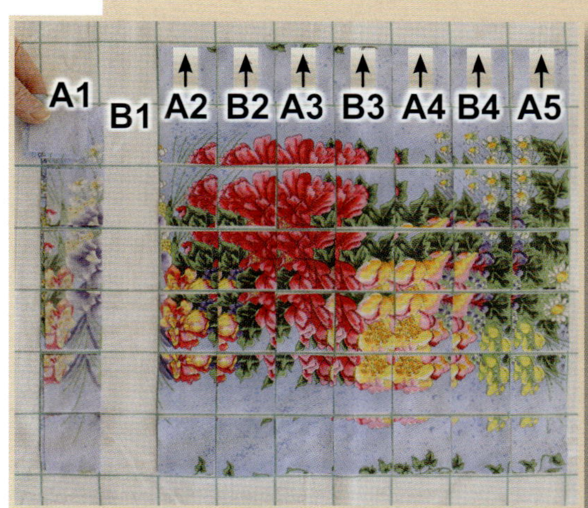

Add the Next Column to Your Stack

1. Put the stack on **top** of **A2** and move down the column, always putting the stack on **top** of the next square.

2. You may sew these columns together or continue picking up the squares. See the Shattered Note.

3. Move to the top of the next column, here marked **B2**, and move down the column, always putting the stack on **top** of the next square.

4. Pick up all the columns, always beginning at the top of the column, moving down, and putting the stack on **top** of the next square.

Once you have collected the squares in one stack, you are ready to sew.

Is Your Project Large?

If your project is large, you may only want to pick up a column or two at a time, instead of all the squares at once. This way, there is less chance that the direction of the squares will change.

Sew the Columns into Rows

You have reached the bottom of the column when you see the arrow on a square showing you the next top row.

1. Put the stack to the **right** of the sewing foot to easily flip the squares to sew.

2. Take the top two flipped square pairs and stitch a ¼-inch seam or less on the right side. *Do not cut the thread.*

3. Take the next two square pairs and stitch right sides together. *Do not cut the thread.*

4. Continue taking the square pairs and stitching right sides together. *Do not cut the thread.*

   Once you have finished sewing the flipped squares (columns 1 and 2), you have reached the bottom of your columns.

5. Cut the machine threads.

6. Open the stitched pairs and check them to make sure they are facing in the same direction. As shown here, columns 1 and 2 are sewn together and open so you see the arrows at the top.

Sew the Third Column into Rows

1. Take the top square from the stack, put it on **top** of the stitched arrow square (arrows and right sides together), and sew together. *Do not cut the thread.*

2. Continue taking each square from the stack and sewing it to each square in the stitched columns.

3. Once you reach the **end**, cut the machine thread, open the sewn squares, and examine them to ensure they are facing in the same direction. Here, you see all the squares sewn together with a few stitches.

4. Press each row of seams in an alternate direction so that the top row faces left, the next row faces right, the next row left, and so on. Be careful not to stretch the squares.

Each row is held together with a few stitches.

Join the Rows

To make your project lie flat without seams bulging, sew and press seams in opposite directions.

1. Beginning with the **top two** rows, sew the rows together alternating the seams.

2. Press each row of seams in the opposite direction. Be careful not to stretch or pull the fabric.

   - Top row seams to the **left**

   - Next row of seams to the **right**

   - Next row of seams to the **left**, and so on

One row seam facing left and the other facing right

Notice the seams of one row face one direction and the seams of the next row face the other direction.

Congratulations!
You have finished Shattering and Sewing an image.
Now let's complete the project by making a placemat.

Make a Placemat

To make a placemat, add borders, backing, and a binding to the Shattered Image.

Follow these easy steps:

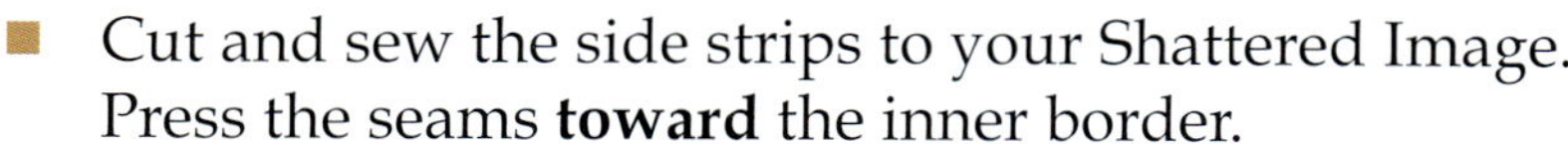

1. **Trim the Edges.** Using a ruler and rotary cutter, trim all sides of the Shattered Image.

2. **Cut Inner Border Strips.** To make a ½-inch border, cut 4 inner border strips 1 x 15 inches long.

   - Cut and sew the side strips to your Shattered Image. Press the seams **toward** the inner border.

   - Cut and sew the top and bottom strips to the Shattered Image. Press the seams **toward** the inner border.

Inner Border

3. **Cut Outer Border Strips.** To make a 1½-inch border, cut 4 outer border strips 2 x 18 inches long.

   - Cut and sew the side strips to the outer border. Press the seams **toward** the outer border.

   - Cut and sew the top and bottom strips to the inner border. Press the seams **toward** the outer border.

Outer Border

4. **Add Batting.** Measure and cut batting to fit the Shattered Image with borders.

5. **Add Backing.** Measure and cut backing material to finish the back. If you want to add your fifth repeat to the back, then frame the original image by cutting border strips to fit the the same dimension as the front.

Backing

Batting

6. **Prepare to Quilt.** Pin the layers (top, batting, and backing) together. You can use any quilt design – the easiest is the meandering stitch.

7. **Add the Binding.** Use the same fabric as your outer border or accent it with a contrasting binding. You can make it wide or narrow – no rule!

- For a ½-inch border, cut two 2 x 44-inch strips and sew them together to make one long strip.

- Fold the strip in half lengthwise, and press.

- Sew both edges to the front of the quilted placemat, as shown.

- Fold the binding over, and hand-stitch the folded side to the back.

Let someone admire your creation!

*Go to **Chapter 3** to see more projects.*

Ideas Gallery

A Rose is a Rose is a Rose

by Carol Juillerat

Carol selected fabric with a plaid background, which adds interest to the piece for her 2-inch squares. The Shattered Image is quilted with a meandering stitch; the green border is quilted in a traditional checkerboard stitch.

Finished size: 20 x 23 inches

The 4-repeat samples in this chapter may give you ideas for your own projects. Some of these samples were completed by students in my classes, so these projects are their first using this technique.

La Rosa

by Linda Bracco

Linda chose a floral design with an interesting background for her first project. Using 2-inch squares, she made a beautiful centerpiece for a small table.

Finished size: 11½ x 15 inches

Flipping Peonies

by Patricia Faust

Pat's first project is a table runner that cleverly arranged the original and Shattered Image so that you can see both images from any view. Because of the lack of material, Pat worked in incredible fractions. The square size is 1¾ inches.

Finished size: 16 x 32 inches

Autumn Extended

by Leslie Sei

Leslie used a bordered fabric to make an autumn table runner. She chose to remove the original gold border and shatter only the flowers in 2-inch squares. Then she sewed the gold border back, using it to frame the Shattered Image center.

Finished size: 15 x 42 inches

Finished size: 18½ inches across

Sweet Dreams

by Connie Mantini

Instead of sewing the 4-repeat, 2-inch squares together, I used Steam-a-Seam2® to attach the squares to the background, which now looks like a grid. The grid is different widths, and each strip of the fish is slightly higher or lower than the others. The fish pillow shows the original 12-inch image from head to tail fin.

My cat, Beannie, was very possessive about her new bed. This photo shows the least amount of cat during our battle for the bed!

Shimmering Toile

by Juanita Tower

Juanita selected a winter-scene toile to shatter, which gave it movement and a cold feeling. She made good use of all of the fabric for her lap quilt using 2-inch squares. This quilt took 3rd place in the 2008 Washoe County Fair.

Finished size: 64½ x 49½ inches

Juicy Grapes

by Connie Mantini

I made this 4-repeat wall hanging from cotton fabric using 3-inch squares.

Finished size: 28 x 28 inches

One, Two, Many

by Connie Mantini

I cut the template into a parallelogram and then cut the 2-inch squares. Working at a tilt had its own challenges… I felt like I had one too many because I constantly had to refer to my original to ensure the squares were not twisted!

Finished size: 18½ x 12½ inches

Playing Coy

by Juanita Tower

Using one fabric, Juanita made this lap quilt by finding 3 different focal points to shatter into 2-inch squares. She also made matching pillows.

Finished size: 66 x 51½ inches

Blooming Beauties

by Karen Kilgore

Karen is an experienced quilter who created this rose-mantic lap quilt. She took two different original image roses approximately 8 x 8 inches, shattered them, and then added one more Shattered Image rose in the center.

Finished size: 45 x 45 inches

Finished size: 30 x 39 inches

Halloween Shake-Up

by Connie Mantini

With this Halloween border fabric showing large pumpkins on the bottom and small bats on the top, what square size would you use?

Well, how about 2 x 3-inch rectangles for the top connected to 3-inch squares on the bottom? When you sew the squares and rectangles together you will get a line, as I did (see arrow above).

I wanted to hide the line, so I followed one of Ellen's suggestions and added a grid to cover this experiment. The web grid created a new illusion.

*See **Chapter 5** for a list of all of Ellen's **Suggestions**.*

CHAPTER 4

Beyond Basics

9-Repeat

So far, you have made a 4-repeat Shattered Image. Now you can take this technique to the next level, using 9 or 16 repeats.

The steps are similar to the 4-repeat:

- Choose a focal point and image size.

- Decide on your square size.

- Cut at least 9 repeats of the image (or make 9 copies of the worksheet on page 84).

- Cut an extra repeat if you want to put an original on the back of your project.

Anchor and Offset Squares

The 9-repeat variation adds 1 more Offset than the 4-repeat, so now you are cutting:

- 1 Anchor (A1)

- 2 Offset squares that expand the image to the side, bottom, and corner

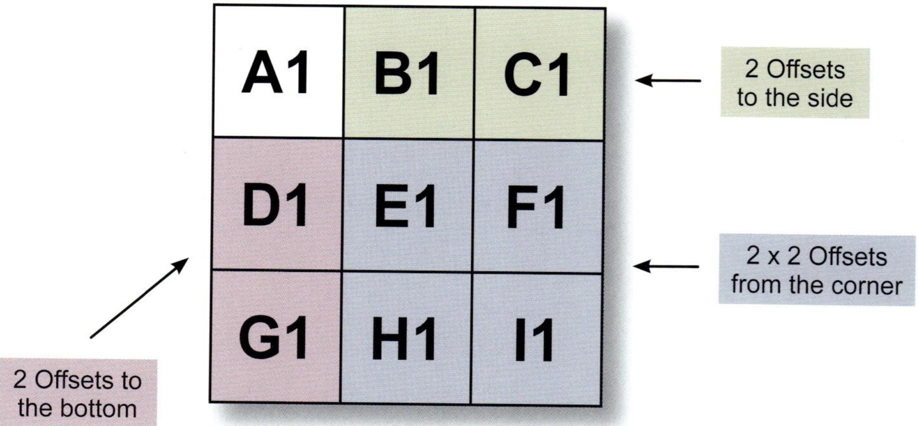

Repeat A

For this 9-repeat, the image size is 6 x 9 inches and the square size is 3 inches – no fractions for me!

1. Spread out your **grid** fabric on a separate work area.

2. Orient all your repeats to face the same direction.

3. Put 1 repeat on the cutting mat.

4. Cut repeat A into squares as you did for the 4-repeat Anchor squares.

5. Cut 3 pieces of tape. Draw an arrow on each piece, and put the tape on each **top** row square to identify the direction of your image.

6. Pick up the squares as you did for the 4-repeat.

7. Place these squares on the grid, in the **A**-designated spaces, to match the diagram.

Image size: 9 x 6 inches
Square size: 3 inches

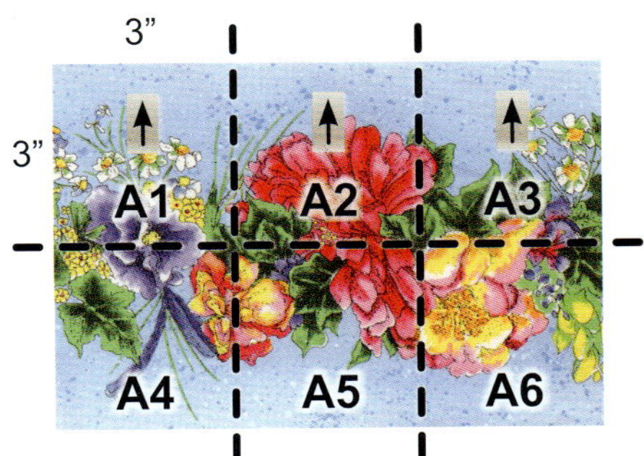

Repeat B

1. Adjust image repeat **B** to create the Offset by trimming:

    - 1 inch from the **left** side

    - 2 inches from the **right** side

2. With the sides trimmed, cut four 3-inch squares.

3. Cut 2 pieces of tape. Draw an arrow on each, and put the tape on the **top** row squares.

4. Pick up the squares and place them in the **B**-designated spaces to match the diagram.

A1	B1		A2	B2		A3
A4	B3		A5	B4		A6

Repeat C

1. Adjust image repeat **C** to create the Offset by trimming:

    - 2 inches from the **left** side

    - 1 inch from the **right** side

2. With the sides trimmed, cut four 3-inch squares.

3. Cut 2 pieces of tape. Draw an arrow on each, and put the tape on the **top** row squares.

4. Pick up the squares and place them in the **C-**designated spaces.

Repeat D

1. Adjust image repeat **D** to create the Offset by trimming:

    - 1 inch from the **top**

    - 2 inches from the **bottom**

Notice that in the 9-repeat, C is placed in a different location than in the 4-repeat.

A1	B1	**C1**	A2	B2	**C2**	A3
D1			**D2**			**D3**
A4	B3	**C3**	A5	B4	**C4**	A6

2. With the top and bottom trimmed, cut three 3-inch squares.

3. Pick up the squares and place them in the **D**-designated spaces.

Repeat E

1. Adjust image repeat **E** to create the Offset by trimming:

   - 1 inch from the **top**
   - 2 inches from the **bottom**
   - 1 inch from the **left** side
   - 2 inches from the **right** side

2. With the top, bottom, and sides trimmed, cut two 3-inch squares.

3. Pick up the squares and place them in the **E**-designated spaces.

Repeat F

1. Adjust image repeat **F** to create the Offset by trimming:

   - 1 inch from the **top**
   - 2 inches from the **bottom**
   - 2 inches from the **left** side
   - 1 inch from the **right** side

2. With the top, bottom, and sides trimmed, cut two 3-inch squares.

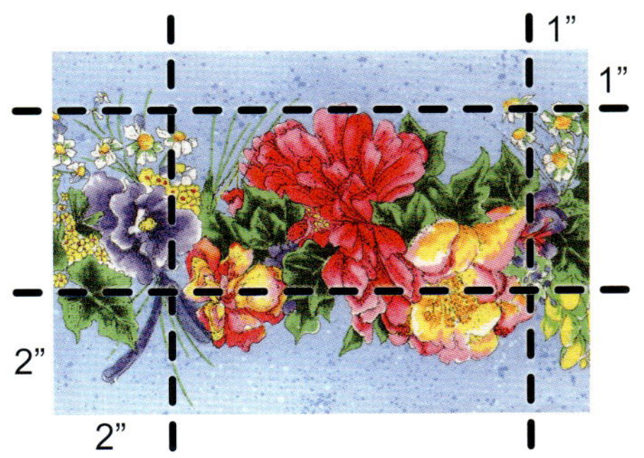

3. Pick up the squares and place them in the **F**-designated spaces.

A1	B1	C1	A2	B2	C2	A3
D1	**E1**	**F1**	D2	**E2**	**F2**	D3
A4	B3	C3	A5	B4	C4	A6

Repeat G

1. Adjust image repeat **G** to create the Offset by trimming:

   - 2 inches from the **top**

   - 1 inch from the **bottom**

2. With the top and bottom trimmed, cut three 3-inch squares.

3. Pick up the squares and place them in the **G**-designated spaces.

Repeat H

1. Adjust image repeat **H** to create the Offset by trimming:

   - 2 inches from the **top**

   - 1 inch from the **bottom**

   - 1 inch from the **left** side

   - 2 inches from the **right** side

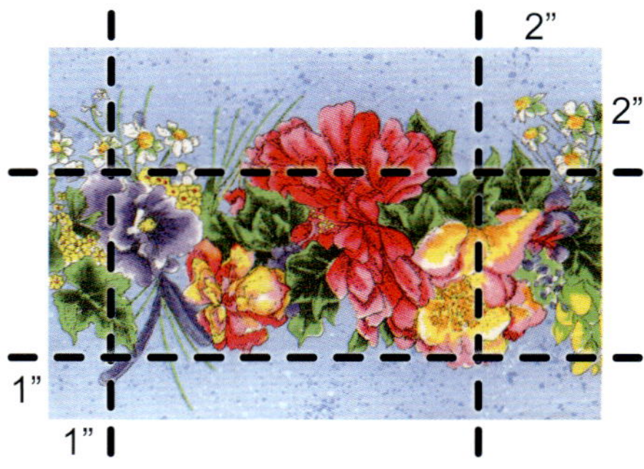

2. With the top and bottom trimmed, cut two 3-inch squares.

3. Pick up the squares and place them in the **H**-designated spaces.

A1	B1	C1	A2	B2	C2	A3
D1	E1	F1	D2	E2	F2	D3
G1	**H1**		**G2**	**H2**		**G3**
A4	B3	C3	A5	B4	C4	A6

Repeat I

1. Adjust image repeat **I** to create the Offset by trimming:

   - 2 inches from the **top**
   - 1 inch from the **bottom**
   - 2 inches from the **left** side
   - 1 inch from the **right** side

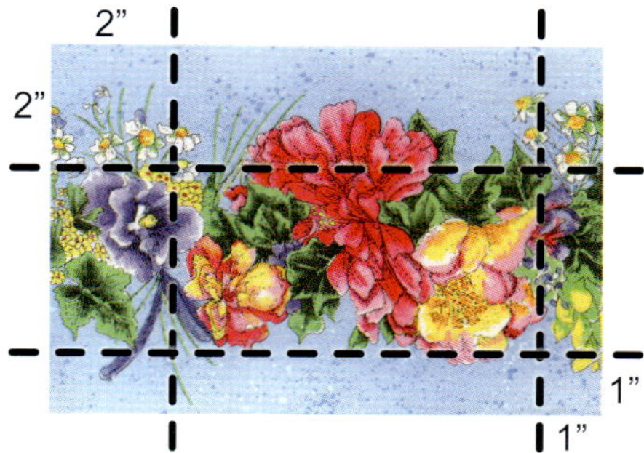

2. With the top, bottom, and sides trimmed, cut two 3-inch squares.

3. Pick up the squares and place them in the **I**-designated spaces.

Pick Up and Sew

Pick up and sew the squares.
Follow the instructions beginning on page 28, *Sew It Together*.

9-Repeat Final Layout

The diagram shows a complete layout of all squares for a 9-repeat Shattered Image.

A1	B1	C1	A2	B2	C2	A3
D1	E1	F1	D2	E2	F2	D3
G1	H1	**I1**	G2	H2	**I2**	G3
A4	B3	C3	A5	B4	C4	A6

A1	B1	C1	A2	B2	C2	A3
D1	E1	F1	D2	E2	F2	D3
G1	H1	I1	G2	H2	I2	G3
A4	B3	C3	A5	B4	C4	A6

Netting Shells

For this 9-repeat, I shattered the *shells* and *netting* using 2-inch squares.

Shells: The first and most obvious is the shell at the center bottom. This shell is the reverse side of the metallic shells.

Netting: At the top of the apron between the 2 metallic shells is a 4½-inch square of netting. I shattered the netting and then used it as a border.

Seeing Stars

Original size: 6 x 14 inches

Finished table runner size:
29 x 12 inches

9-repeat, 2-inch squares

Kaleidoscoped Teddies

The number of Offsets to use depends on the effect you're trying to achieve. Inserting more than 3 Offsets (16-repeat), makes a pretty abstract image out of even the simplest flower or animal, as seen in *Kaleidoscoped Teddies*.

Notice what happens to the teddies' heads and eyes as the image is shattered.

9-repeat
Shattered Image:
14½ x 10 inches

4-repeat
Shattered Image:
10 x 7 inches

Original panel:
8 x 6 inches

16-repeat
Shattered Image:
19 x 12 inches

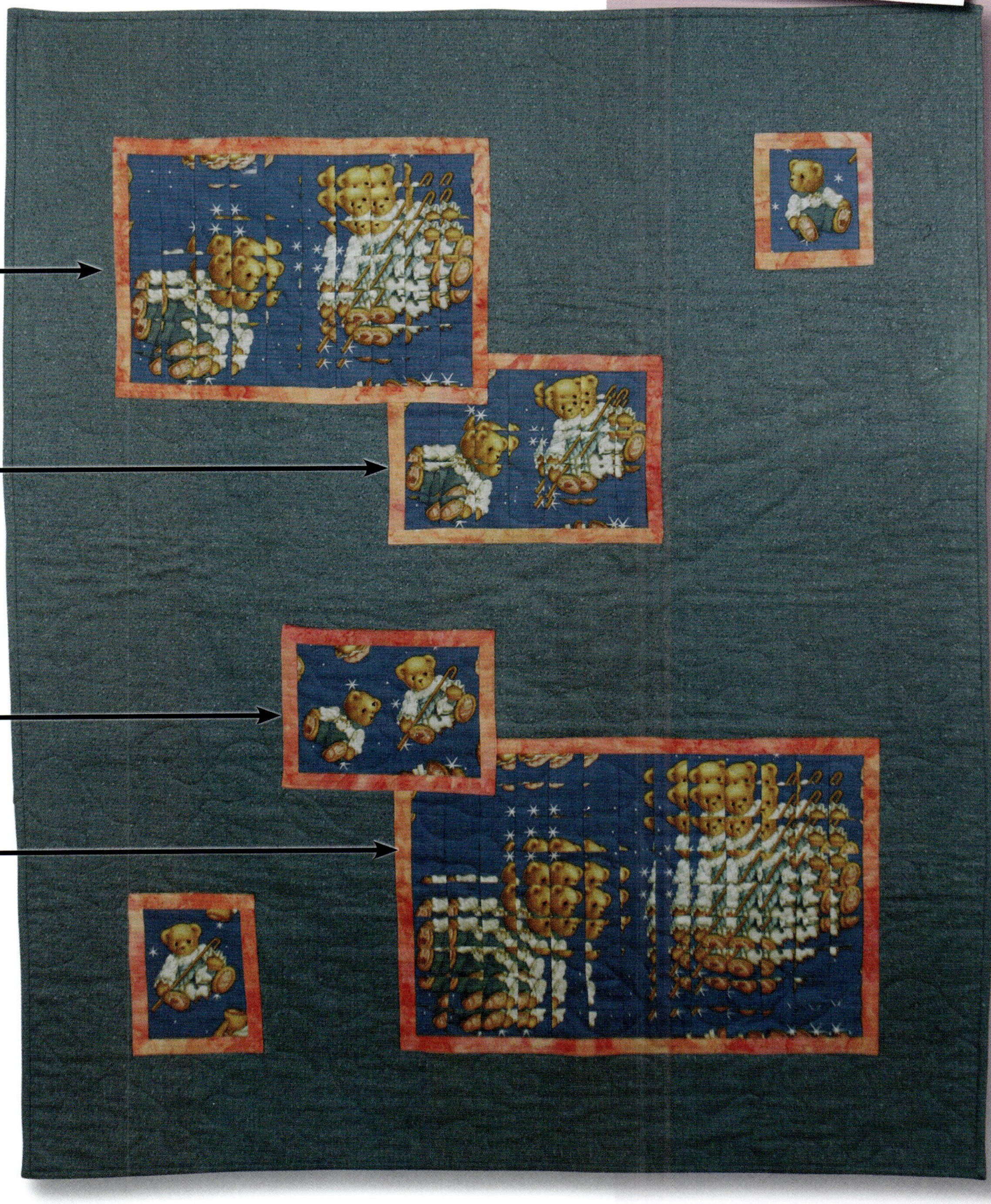

Finished baby quilt size: 40 x 47½ inches

Swimming with Pisces

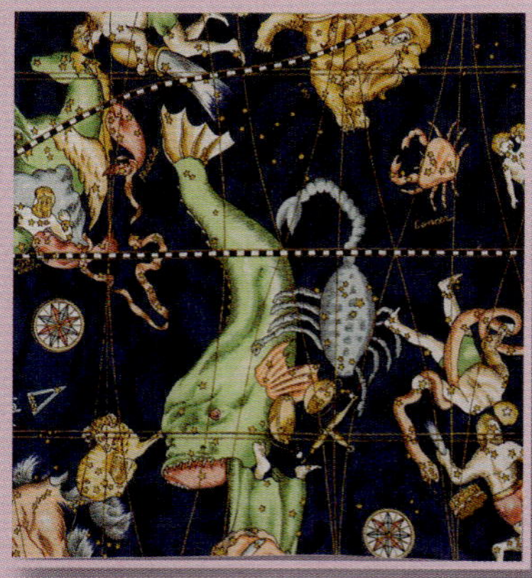

Original size:
9 x 9 inches

Finished pillow size:
24 x 24 inches

16-repeat with
2-inch squares

16-Repeat

Ready to try a 16-repeat variation? This time you will shatter an image by cutting and working with 16 repeats that are labeled A through P. To learn this variation, you can use the 8 x 10-inch worksheet on page 83 or your own fabric. You need enough fabric to cut 16 (or 17) repeats, which results in a very abstract image.

The 16-repeat sample that I am using throughout these instructions has…

- An image size of 8 x 10 inches
- A square size of 2 inches

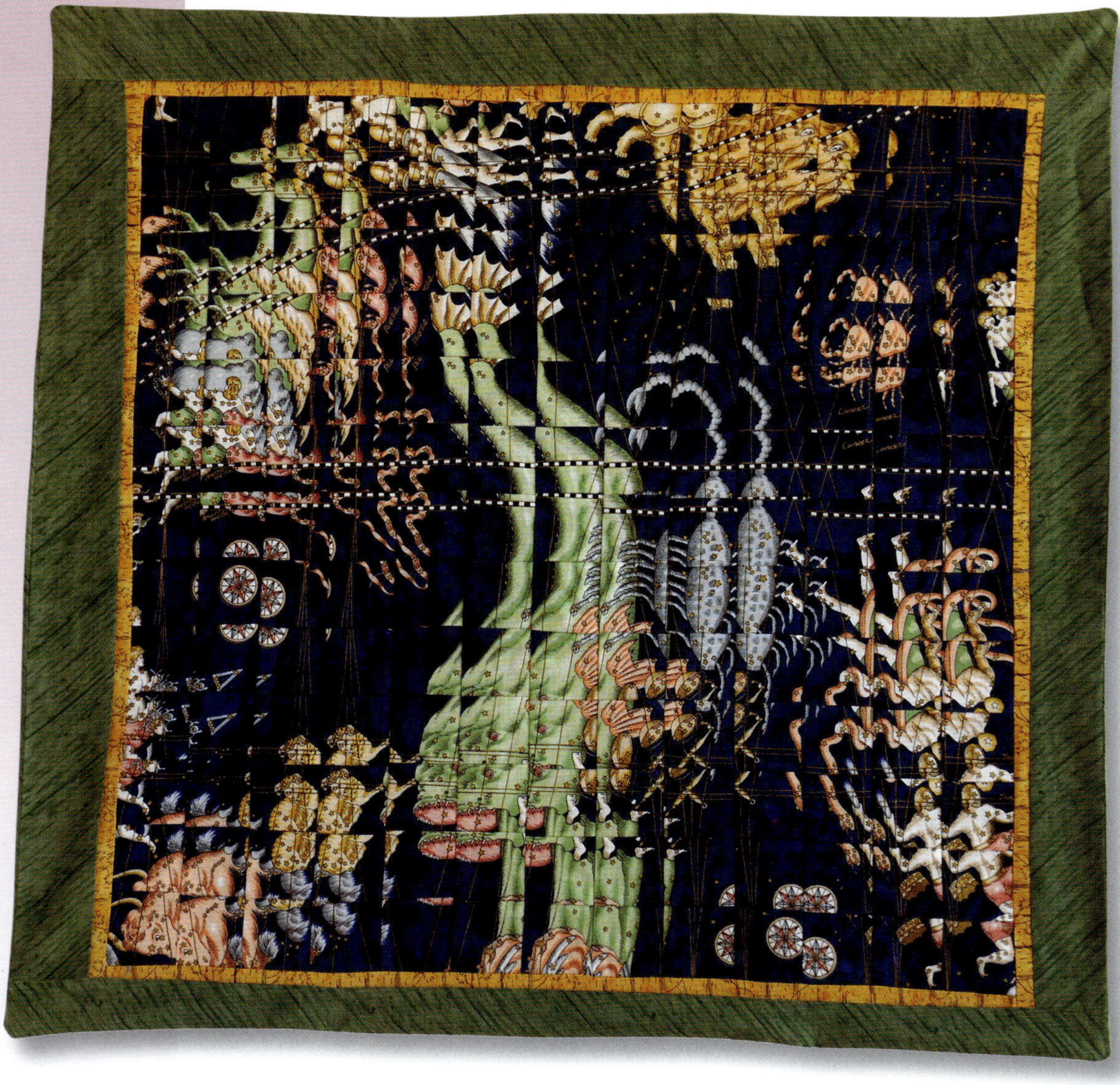

Anchor and Offset Squares

When cutting a 16-repeat, you are cutting:

- 1 Anchor (**A1**)

- 3 Offset squares that expand the image to the side, bottom, and corner

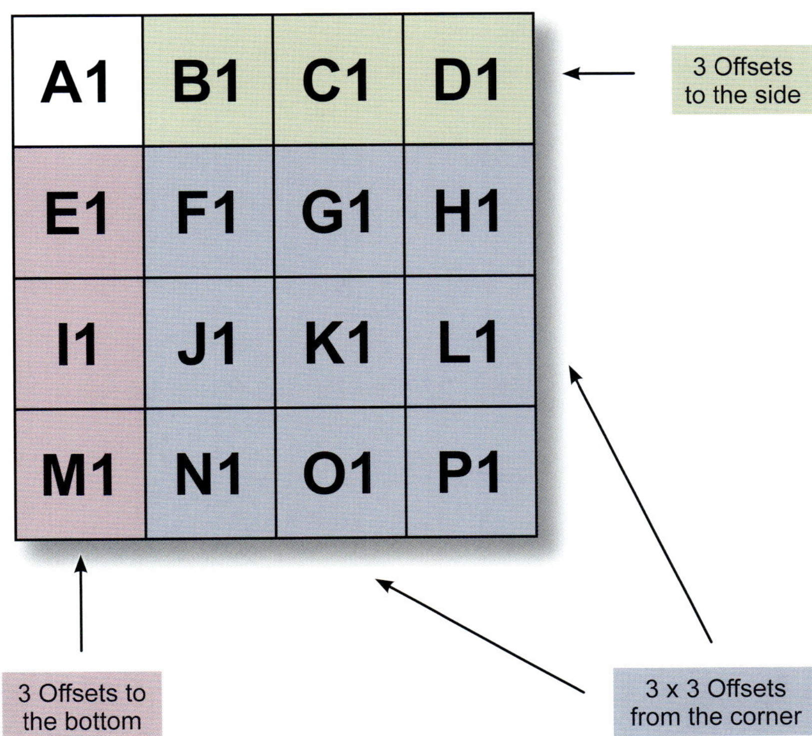

Shattered Note

Trimming Offset Squares

As you have seen, trimming Offsets depends on:

- Square size

- Number of image repeats

When you made the 4-repeat, you trimmed the square size by ½.

When you made the 9-repeat, you trimmed the square size by ⅓.

Now, with the 16-repeat, you will trim each square size by ¼.

Repeat A

1. Spread out your **grid** fabric on a separate work area.

2. Orient all your repeats to face the same direction.

3. Put 1 repeat on the cutting mat.

4. Cut the Anchor repeat (A) into squares as you did for the 4-repeat. In this example, the square size is 2 inches.

5. Draw arrows on 5 pieces of tape. Put them on the **top** row of your squares.

6. Pick up and stack the squares as you did for the 4-repeat.

7. Place these squares in the **A**-designated spaces to match the diagram.

A1	B1	C1	D1	A2	B2	C2	D2	A3	B3	C3	D3	A4	B4	C4	D4	A5
A6	B5	C5	D5	A7	B6	C6	D6	A8	B7	C7	D7	A9	B8	C8	D8	A10
A11	B9	C9	D9	A12	B10	C10	D10	A13	B11	C11	D11	A14	B12	C12	D12	A15
A16	B13	C13	D13	A17	B14	C14	D14	A18	B15	C15	D15	A19	B16	C16	D16	A20

Repeat B

1. Adjust image repeat **B** to create the Offset
    by trimming:

    - ½ inch from the **left** side

    - 1½ inches from the **right** side

2. With the sides trimmed, cut sixteen 2-inch squares.

3. Draw arrows on 4 pieces of tape. Put them on the
    top row squares.

4. Pick up the squares and place them in the
    B-designated spaces.

Repeat C

1. Adjust image repeat **C** to create the Offset by trimming:

    - 1 inch from the **left** side

    - 1 inch from the **right** side

2. With the sides trimmed, cut sixteen 2-inch squares.

3. Draw arrows on 4 pieces of tape. Put them on the **top**
    row squares.

4. Pick up the squares and place them in the
    C-designated spaces.

Repeat D

1. Adjust image repeat **D** to create the Offset by trimming:

    - 1½ inches from the **left** side

    - ½ inch from the **right** side

2. With the sides trimmed, cut sixteen 2-inch squares.

3. Draw arrows on 4 pieces of tape. Put them on the **top**
    row squares.

4. Pick up the squares and place them in the
    D-designated spaces.

Repeat E

You are moving down the first column.

1. Adjust image repeat **E** to create the Offset by trimming:
    - ½ inch from the **top**
    - 1½ inches from the **bottom**

2. With the top and bottom trimmed, cut fifteen 2-inch squares.

3. Pick up the squares and place them in the
    E-designated spaces.

A1	B1	C1	D1	A2	B2	C2	D2	A3	B3	C3	D3	A4	B4	C4	D4	A5
E1	F1	G1	H1	E2	F2	G2	H2	E3	F3	G3	H3	E4	F4	G4	H4	E5
A6	B5	C5	D5	A7	B6	C6	D6	A8	B7	C7	D7	A9	B8	C8	D8	A10
E6	F5	G5	H5	E7	F6	G6	H6	E8	F7	G7	H7	E9	F8	G8	H8	E10
A11	B9	C9	D9	A12	B10	C10	D10	A13	B11	C11	D11	A14	B12	C12	D12	A15
E11	F9	G9	H9	E12	F10	G10	H10	E13	F11	G11	H11	E14	F12	G12	H12	E15
A16	B13	C13	D13	A17	B14	C14	D14	A18	B15	C15	D15	A19	B16	C16	D16	A20

Repeat F

You are moving across the row.

1. Adjust image repeat **F** to create the Offset by trimming:

    - ½ inch from the **top**
    - 1½ inches from the **bottom**
    - ½ inch from the **left** side
    - 1½ inches from the **right** side

2. With all sides trimmed, cut twelve 2-inch squares.

3. Pick up the squares and place them in the **F**-designated spaces.

Repeat G

You are continuing across the row.

1. Adjust image repeat **G** to create the Offset by trimming:

    - ½ inch from the **top**
    - 1½ inches from the **bottom**
    - 1 inch from the **left** side
    - 1 inch from the **right** side

2. With all sides trimmed, cut twelve 2-inch squares.

3. Pick up the squares and place them in the **G**-designated spaces.

Repeat H

You are continuing across the row.

1. Adjust image repeat **H** to create the Offset by trimming:

    - ½ inch from the **top**
    - 1½ inches from the **bottom**
    - 1½ inches from the **left** side
    - ½ inch from the **right** side

2. With all sides trimmed, cut twelve 2-inch squares.

3. Pick up the squares and place them in the **H**-designated spaces.

Repeat I

You are moving down the first column again.

1. Adjust image repeat **I** to create the Offset by trimming:
    - 1 inch from the **top**
    - 1 inch from the **bottom**

2. With the top and bottom trimmed, cut fifteen 2-inch squares.

3. Pick up the squares and place them in the
    I-designated spaces.

A1	B1	C1	D1	A2	B2	C2	D2	A3	B3	C3	D3	A4	B4	C4	D4	A5
E1	F1	G1	H1	E2	F2	G2	H2	E3	F3	G3	H3	E4	F4	G4	H4	E5
I1	J1	K1	L1	I2	J2	K2	L2	I3	J3	K3	L3	I4	J4	K4	L4	I5
A6	B5	C5	D5	A7	B6	C6	D6	A8	B7	C7	D7	A9	B8	C8	D8	A10
E6	F5	G5	H5	E7	F6	G6	H6	E8	F7	G7	H7	E9	F8	G8	H8	E10
I6	J5	K5	L5	I7	J6	K6	L6	I8	J7	K7	L7	I9	J8	K8	L8	I10
A11	B9	C9	D9	A12	B10	C10	D10	A13	B11	C11	D11	A14	B12	C12	D12	A15
E11	F9	G9	H9	E12	F10	G10	H10	E13	F11	G11	H11	E14	F12	G12	H12	E15
I11	J9	K9	L9	I12	J10	K10	L10	I13	J11	K11	L11	I14	J12	K12	L12	I15
A16	B13	C13	D13	A17	B14	C14	D14	A18	B15	C15	D15	A19	B16	C16	D16	A20

Repeat J

You are moving across the row.

1. Adjust image repeat **J** to create the Offset
    by trimming:

    - 1 inch from the **top**

    - 1 inch from the **bottom**

    - ½ inch from the **left** side

    - 1½ inches from the **right** side

2. With all sides trimmed, cut twelve 2-inch squares.

3. Pick up the squares and place them in the
    J-designated spaces.

Repeat K

You are continuing across the row.

1. Adjust image repeat **K** to create the Offset by trimming:

    - 1 inch from the **top**

    - 1 inch from the **bottom**

    - 1 inch from the **left** side

    - 1 inch from the **right** side

2. With all sides trimmed, cut twelve 2-inch squares.

3. Pick up the squares and place them in the
    K-designated spaces.

Repeat L

You are continuing across the row.

1. Adjust image repeat **L** to create the Offset by trimming:

    - 1 inch from the **top**

    - 1 inch from the **bottom**

    - 1½ inches from the **left** side

    - ½ inch from the **right** side

2. With all sides trimmed, cut twelve 2-inch squares.

3. Pick up the squares and place them in the
    L-designated spaces.

Repeat M

You are moving down the first column again.

1. Adjust image repeat **M** to create the Offset by trimming:
    - 1½ inches from the **top**
    - ½ inch from the **bottom**

2. With the top and bottom trimmed, cut fifteen 2-inch squares.

3. Pick up the squares and place them in the
    M-designated spaces.

A1	B1	C1	D1	A2	B2	C2	D2	A3	B3	C3	D3	A4	B4	C4	D4	A5
E1	F1	G1	H1	E2	F2	G2	H2	E3	F3	G3	H3	E4	F4	G4	H4	E5
I1	J1	K1	L1	I2	J2	K2	L2	I3	J3	K3	L3	I4	J4	K4	L4	I5
M1	N1	O1	P1	M2	N2	O2	P2	M3	N3	O3	P3	M4	N4	O4	P4	M5
A6	B5	C5	D5	A7	B6	C6	D6	A8	B7	C7	D7	A9	B8	C8	D8	A10
E6	F5	G5	H5	E7	F6	G6	H6	E8	F7	G7	H7	E9	F8	G8	H8	E10
I6	J5	K5	L5	I7	J6	K6	L6	I8	J7	K7	L7	I9	J8	K8	L8	I10
M6	N5	O5	P5	M7	N6	O6	P6	M8	N7	O7	P7	M9	N8	O8	P8	M10
A11	B9	C9	D9	A12	B10	C10	D10	A13	B11	C11	D11	A14	B12	C12	D12	A15
E11	F9	G9	H9	E12	F10	G10	H10	E13	F11	G11	H11	E14	F12	G12	H12	E15
I11	J9	K9	L9	I12	J10	K10	L10	I13	J11	K11	L11	I14	J12	K12	L12	I15
M11	N9	O9	P9	M12	N10	O10	P10	M13	N11	O11	P11	M14	N12	O12	P12	M15
A16	B13	C13	D13	A17	B14	C14	D14	A18	B15	C15	D15	A19	B16	C16	D16	A20

Repeat N

You are moving across the row.

1. Adjust image repeat **N** to create the Offset by trimming:

   - 1½ inches from the **top**
   - ½ inch from the **bottom**
   - ½ inch from the **left** side
   - 1½ inches from the **right** side

2. With all sides trimmed, cut twelve 2-inch squares.

3. Pick up the squares and place them in the **N**-designated spaces.

Repeat O

You are continuing across the row.

1. Adjust image repeat **O** to create the Offset by trimming:

   - 1½ inches from the **top**
   - ½ inch from the **bottom**
   - 1 inch from the **left** side
   - 1 inch from the **right** side

2. With all sides trimmed, cut twelve 2-inch squares.

3. Pick up the squares and place them in the **O**-designated spaces.

Repeat P

You are continuing across the row.

1. Adjust image repeat **P** to create the Offset by trimming:

   - 1½ inches from the **top**
   - ½ inch from the **bottom**
   - 1½ inches from the **left** side
   - ½ inch from the **right** side

2. With all sides trimmed, cut twelve 2-inch squares.

3. Pick up the squares and place them in the **P**-designated spaces.

16-Repeat Final Layout

The diagram shows a complete layout of all squares for a
16-repeat Shattered Image.

Pick Up and Sew

Pick up and sew the squares.
Follow the instructions beginning on page 28, *Sew It Together*.

A1	B1	C1	D1	A2	B2	C2	D2	A3	B3	C3	D3	A4	B4	C4	D4	A5
E1	F1	G1	H1	E2	F2	G2	H2	E3	F3	G3	H3	E4	F4	G4	H4	E5
I1	J1	K1	L1	I2	J2	K2	L2	I3	J3	K3	L3	I4	J4	K4	L4	I5
M1	N1	O1	P1	M2	N2	O2	P2	M3	N3	O3	P3	M4	N4	O4	P4	M5
A6	B5	C5	D5	A7	B6	C6	D6	A8	B7	C7	D7	A9	B8	C8	D8	A10
E6	F5	G5	H5	E7	F6	G6	H6	E8	F7	G7	H7	E9	F8	G8	H8	E10
I6	J5	K5	L5	I7	J6	K6	L6	I8	J7	K7	L7	I9	J8	K8	L8	I10
M6	N5	O6	P5	M7	N6	O6	P6	M8	N7	O7	P7	M9	N8	O8	P8	M10
A11	B9	C9	D9	A12	B10	C10	D10	A13	B11	C11	D11	A14	B12	C12	D12	A15
E11	F9	G9	H9	E12	F10	G10	H10	E13	F11	G11	H11	E14	F12	G12	H12	E15
I11	J9	K9	L9	I12	J10	K10	L10	I13	J11	K11	L11	I14	J12	K12	L12	I15
M11	N9	O9	P9	M12	N10	O10	P10	M13	N12	O11	P11	M14	N12	O12	P12	M15
A16	B13	C13	D13	A17	B14	C14	D14	A18	B15	C15	D15	A19	B16	C16	D16	A20

Glazed Peonies

by Karen Kilgore

Finished tablecloth size: 42 x 42 inches

16 repeats with 2-inch squares

Shattering Mondrian

Finished lap quilt size: 38 x 53 inches

16 repeats with 2-inch squares

Fabric Selection Exceptions

When making the *Shattering Mondrian* lap quilt,
I found that there are exceptions to the guidelines for
selecting fabric. The elements in each of these samples
do not fit the general guidelines listed earlier.

However, they achieved my purpose, which was to add
another dimension to the work of one of my favorite artists.

Also, I quilted this piece using a stitch-in-the-ditch, rather
than a meandering or a pattern. It appeared that this
contemporary piece broke all guidelines. So, it depends
on what you are trying to achieve. There are no rules!

See **Choose Fabric**
on page 10 for
general guidelines.

The largest fish is
1¾ inches long.

The lemons have
no eye rest.

The largest flower is
1¼ inches wide.

CHAPTER 5

Ellen's Gallery

"In my own work, I strive to strike a balance between the idea expressed in a piece, and its overall decorative appeal. I am particularly entranced by pattern, with its underlying repetition; attributes generously provided by printed fabrics. In my pieces, repeat designs manifest themselves in a formal, decorative way, in an expressive, pictorial way, or some combination of the two. A grid supports and organizes how a repeating pattern appears in each piece, sometimes also contributing to its narrative content."

"By integrating form and content in the way I do, I hope to convince [viewers] that textiles are an appropriate medium for expressing my ideas, at the same time as I provide aesthetic pleasure through rich juxtapositions of colour and texture."

Ellen Adams

Ellen began her quilts by accurately drawing the full-size design. She then transferred the reverse image to muslin and hand-appliquéd on the opposite side of the muslin. She combined fabrics such as satins and velvets. She assembled all 3 layers of quilt by hand, doing what was functionally necessary to hold the 3 layers together.

Suggestions

This chapter presents Ellen Adams' Shattered Image projects and her comments about each piece. As you look through, see how many of her suggestions she used to embellish or add illusion to her Shattered Image work.

Grid

Add a grid to "trick the eye into believing that the image beyond the grid is continuous." The thicker the grid, the more prominent it becomes on the quilt; the rounder the grid edges, the less linear the Shattered Image becomes. Ellen suggested varying the grid widths using a narrow grid on one side of the image and increasing the grid width to a thicker grid on the opposite side of the image.

Grids can be created by using:

- Strips of fabric or ribbon placed on top of the project
- Framing each square and adding insets
- Reverse appliqué

Linearity

Disguise linearity by tilting the Shattered Image before placing it on a background, like *Small Craft Warning* on page 78, or by adding frames around each square and arranging individual squares on the background, like *Archaic Remnants* on page 70.

Materials

Use different design materials, such as paper or photographs.

Motifs

Make a custom motif in a fabric collage using abstract, figurative, and/or photo-realistic motifs.

Features

Use a Shattered Image as one component or as the background for an appliqué.

More Offsets

Add more Offsets to further diffuse your image. What about a 25-repeat Shattered Image project, with 1 Anchor and 4 Offsets?

Color

Use different colors of the same motif.

Non-Square Units

Create Shattered Images from basic units other than squares, such as rectangles, parallelograms, and so on.

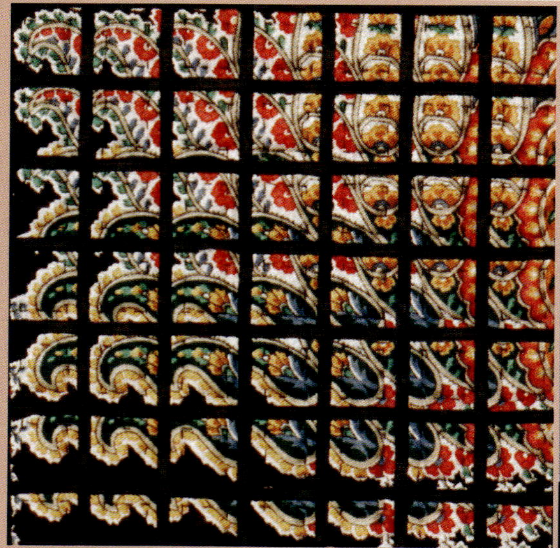

Shattered Paisley

"When the Shattered Image squares are arranged on the grid fabric, you can add grid lines that are even in width and distance or you can begin with a line that is smaller on one side and gradually larger as you move across the image. You can use fabric, ribbon, or any other medium to make your grid accent."

Ellen Adams

Made using natural and synthetic fabrics, polyester ribbon, polyester filling, and cotton backing.

Finished size:
22 x 15 inches

1990

This is Ellen's first Shattered Image work, which was on display at the Cambridge Library and Gallery in Ontario, Canada. The library acquired this piece and it remains as part of their permanent collection.

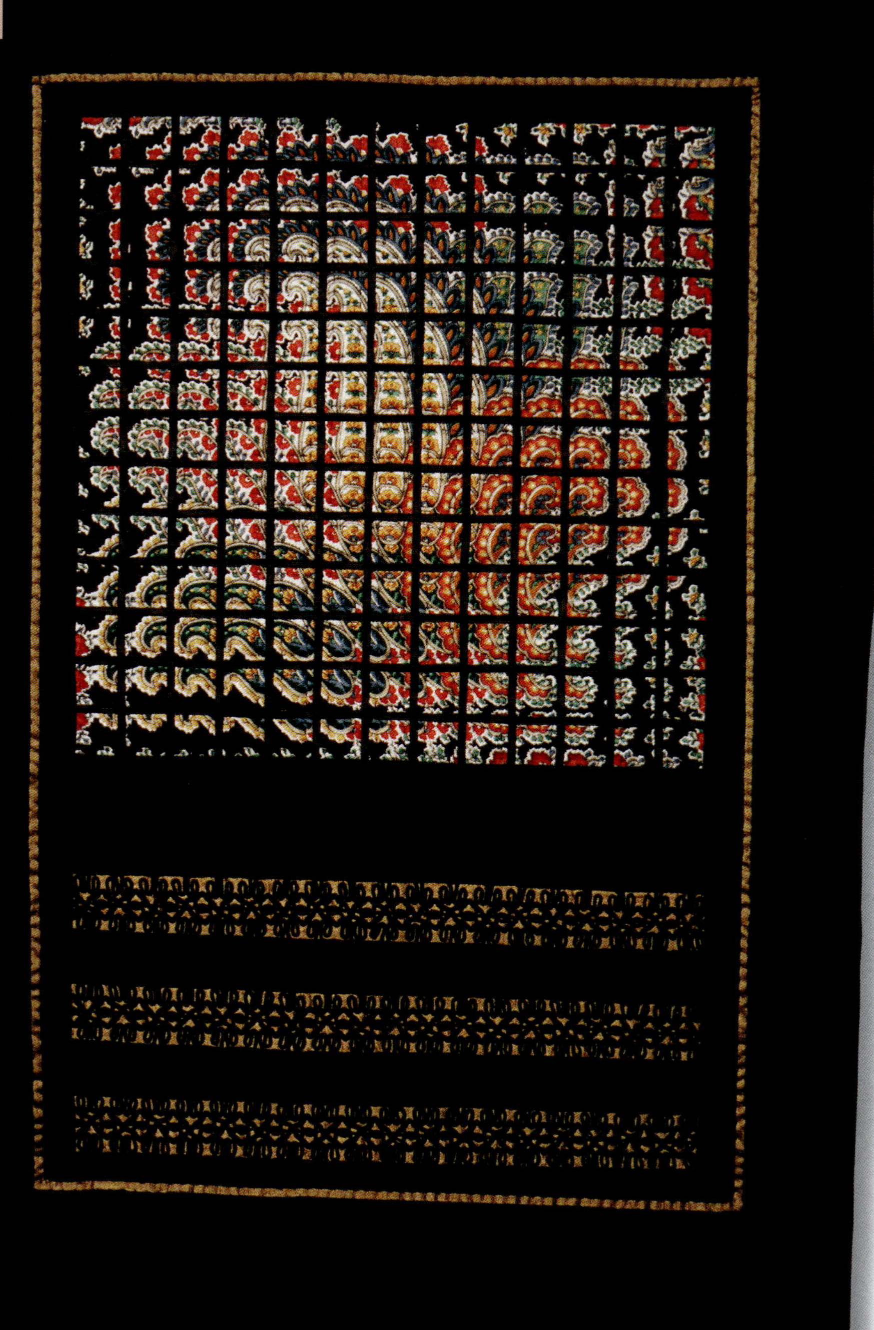

Fish Looking for the Same Food

*"**Fish Looking for the Same Food** is assembled from
sixteen copies [repeats] of a print fabric motif, cut up
and arranged according to a simple set of rules. The
result is a stretched, or exploded version of the motif;
small areas of colour get played out over a wider
field, and the iterations in the design set up a rhythm
that reminds me of a swirling school of fish."*

Ellen Adams

Made using
natural and
synthetic fabrics,
polyester ribbon,
polyester filling,
and cotton
backing.

Finished size:
62 x 62 inches

1991

*This is an example of using a grid; but also notice the inset squares,
which add another visual entity. The combination breaks the linearity.*

Self Portrait

"*Self Portrait* is assembled from sixteen heat transfer copies of a head and shoulders photograph, resulting in an unconventional view through a window. The superimposed grid over the array of squares masks the interruptions in the design and encourages the viewer to perceive a continuous and coherent image."

Ellen Adams

The photo of Ellen was taken in a blue-period pose.

Made using natural and synthetic fabrics, polyester ribbon, photo transfers, polyester filling, and cotton backing.

Finished size:
41 x 80 inches

1992

Common Ground

*This is an
example of using
a ribbon as a grid.*

Archaic Remnants

"*Archaic Remnants* is assembled from sixteen identical collages containing thirty printed fabrics. The title implies using up old leftovers, as well as referring to those puzzling but somehow familiar images that crop up in dreams, that Jungian psychologists ascribe to our collective unconscious."

Ellen Adams

This is Ellen's original collage.

Estimated original size:
24 x 24 inches

*Ellen based her design on a portion of Henri Rousseau's 1910 painting, **The Dream**. From the full painting, she selected the segment with tigers, then created a collage using 30 remnants. She cut the collages into 6-inch squares.*

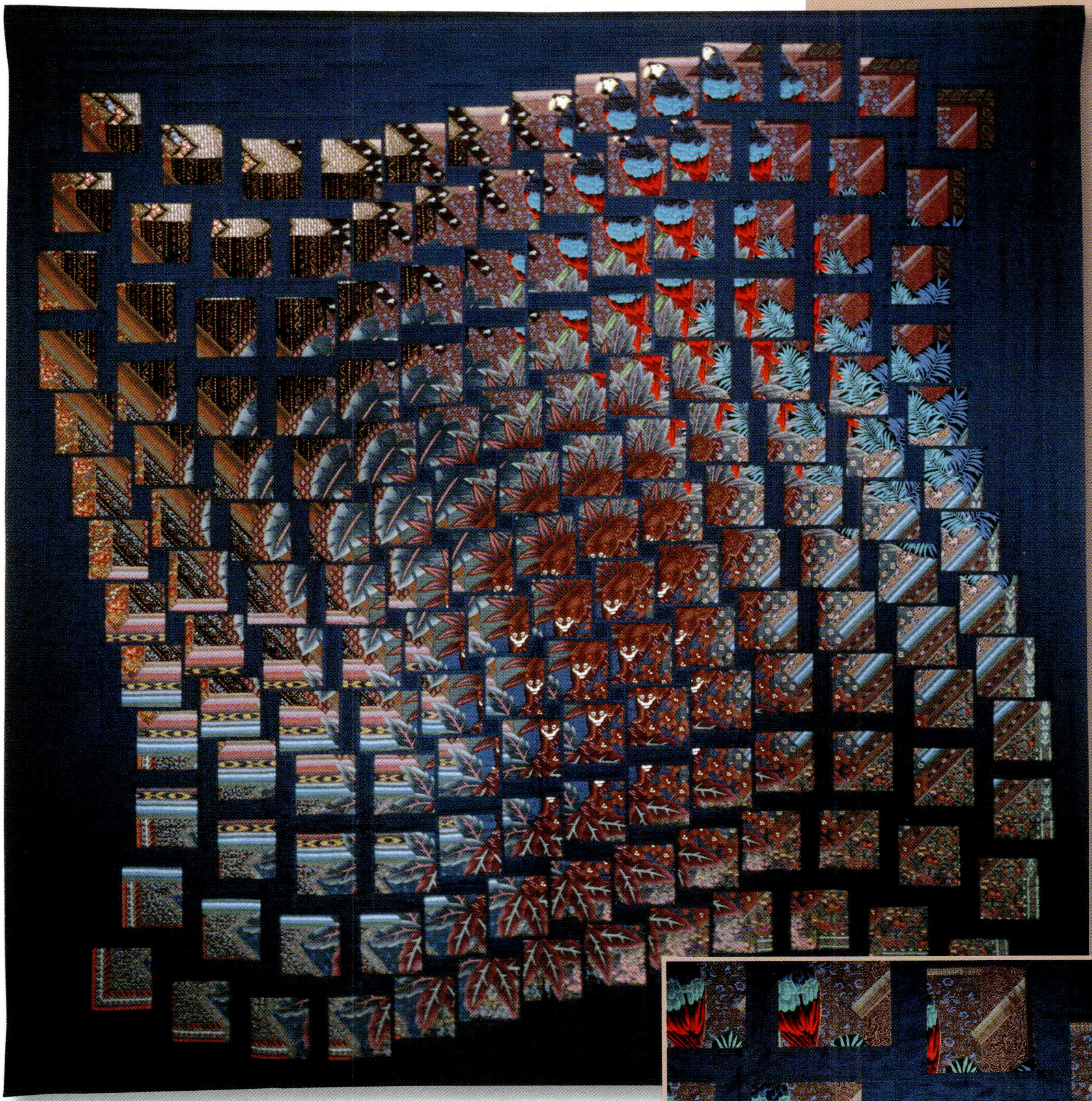

Parrots show
detail of top right.

Made using natural and
synthetic fabrics, polyester
ribbon, polyester filling, and
cotton backing.

Finished size:
104½ x 104½ inches

1994

Tigers show
detail of middle.

White Tiger

Made using cotton and cotton blend fabrics, polyester filling, and cotton backing.

Finished size: 53½ x 77 inches

1994

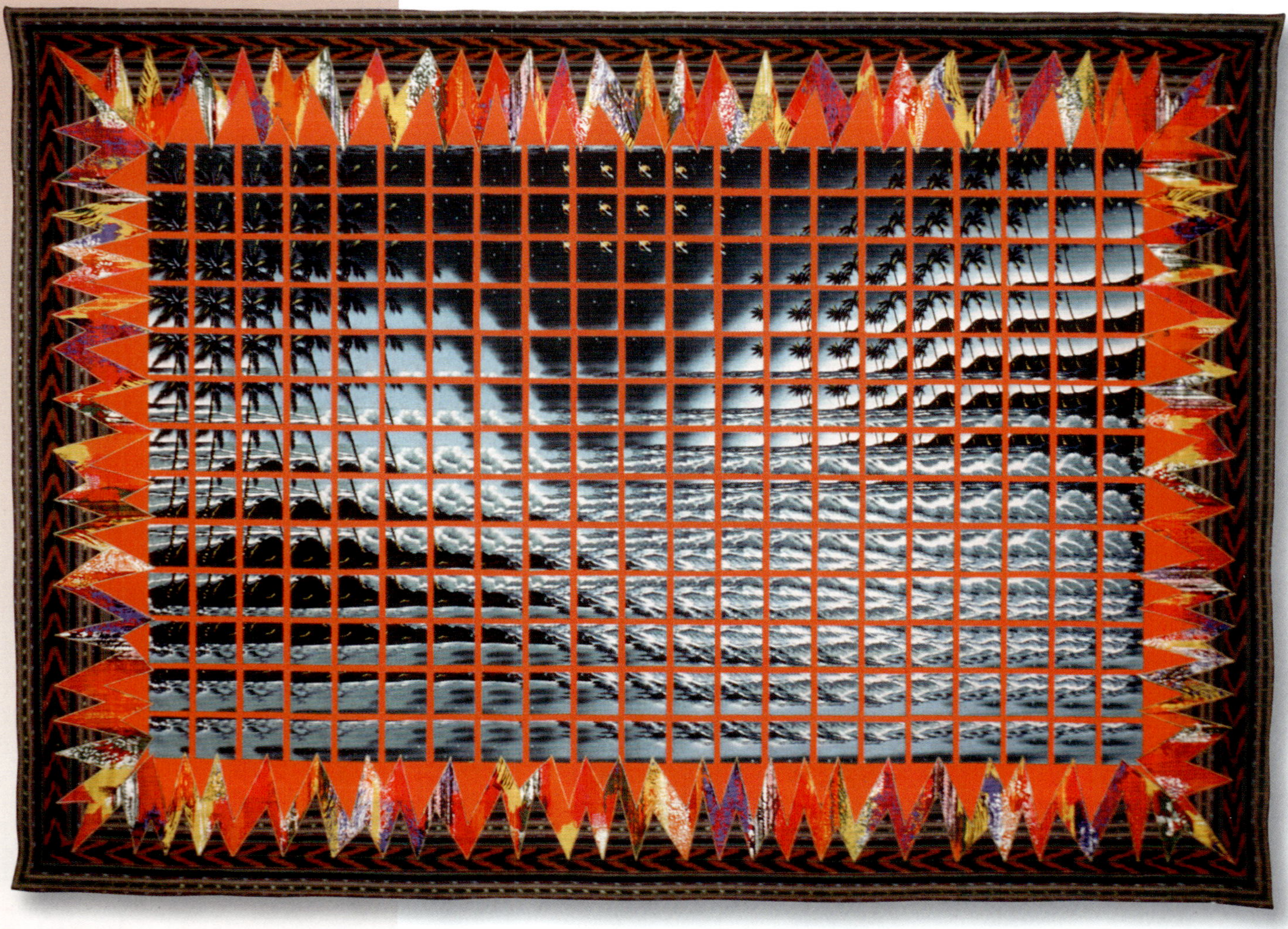

*"**White Tiger** is assembled from sixteen copies of a fabric print image of waves crashing on a tropical beach. In this stretched and enlarged version, the staccato rhythm set up by the little repetitions within the waves emphasizes the power in the water. This allusion to energy is also manifested by the fiery border. In Chinese mythology, the fusion of the two elements fire and water is expressed by the mystic being, White Tiger."*

Ellen Adams

This piece shows how you can play with recognizable images (palm trees and ocean) to make a more abstract pattern.

Sixteen Cats and Nine Fleas

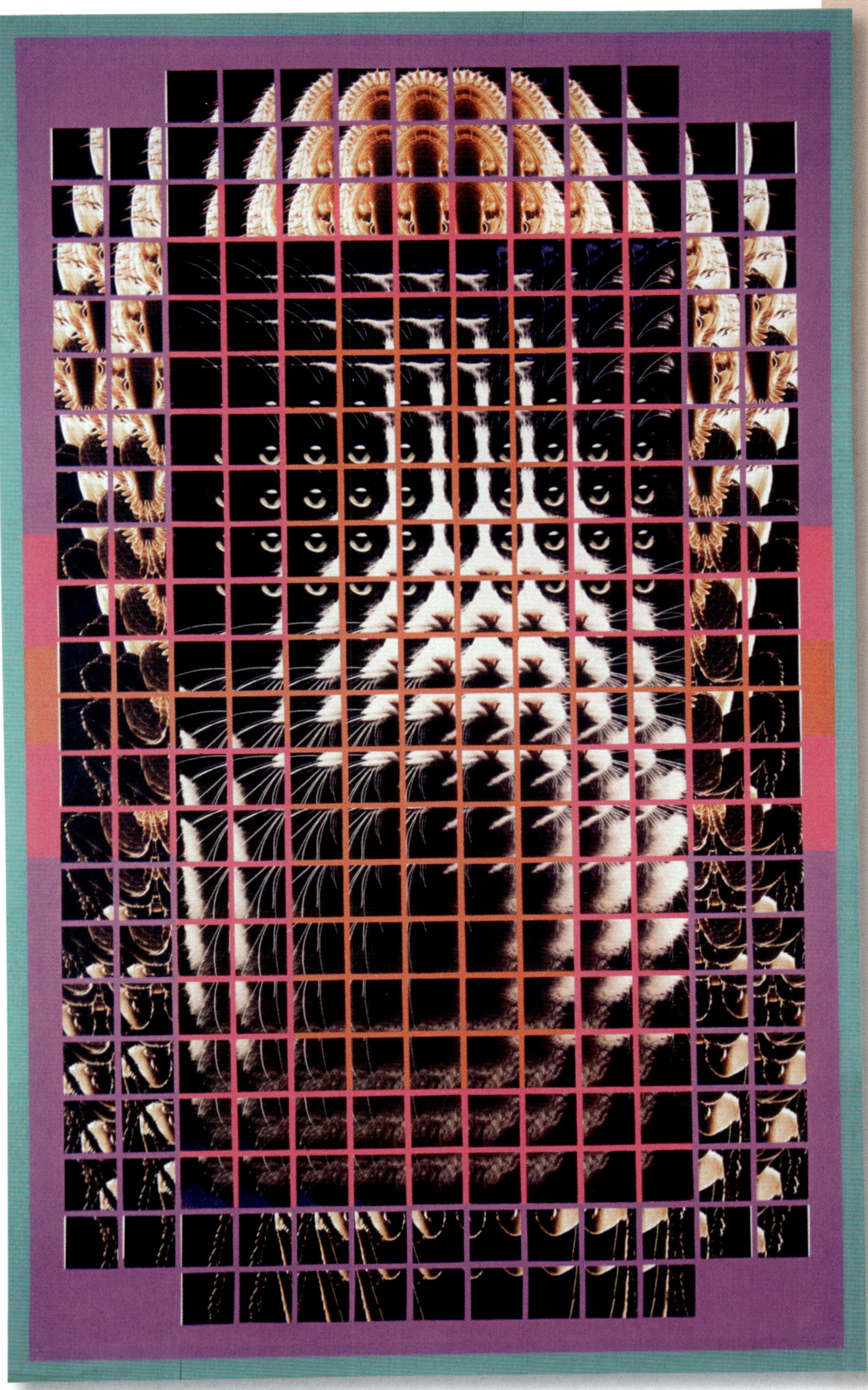

Cotton and cotton-blend fabrics, photo transfers, polyester filling, and cotton backing.

Finished size:
61 x 46 inches

1996

Ellen used iron-on transfer photocopies of a picture she took in a London park. She ironed each square onto fabric, leaving a border to provide a seam allowance and grid.

Memory Tracings

"**Memory Tracings** sets up a mood of nostalgia and loss. Through my choice of colours, and by presenting the image in a very fragmented form, I have tried to suggest some of the frustration I feel when trying to conjure up a place from the past in my mind's eye. What I get is imperfect recall, where some parts are recognizable, but others are hazy or mysterious, as in this view of a tangled garden in an old arbour. One is left yearning for more clarity and coherence, but also grateful for an enduring sense of place."

Ellen Adams

Kashmiri Garden

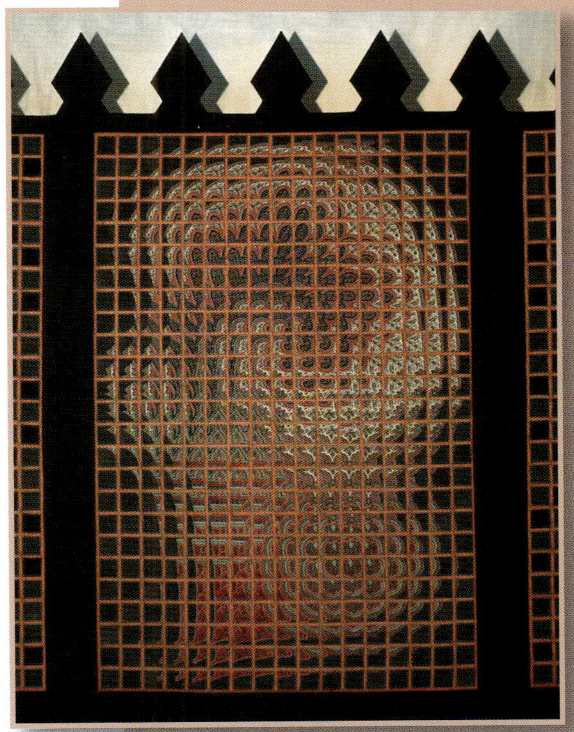

Made using natural and synthetic fabrics, polyester filling, and cotton backing.

Finished size:
121 x 50 inches

1996

This piece was commissioned for the stairwell of a private house, where the whole piece could be seen from the top of the stairs and the lower portion could be examined more closely from the landing half-way.

Ellen used the Shattered Image technique between the lattices.

Srinagar, Kashmir

"*Srinagar, Kashimir* is assembled from sixteen heat transfer copies of a photograph showing a waterway in the old city of Srinagar. The massive, though decorative grid obscuring much of the image alludes to how circumscribed the view of anything can be for women…"

Ellen Adams

The grid was created by cutting out parts of fabric and leaving the background fabric to become the grid (a reverse appliqué).

Made from natural and synthetic fabrics, photo transfers, glass-seed beads, cotton embroidery floss, and cotton filling and backing.

Finished size:
32½ x 48 inches

1997

Passing Through

Made using natural and synthetic fabrics, polyester ribbon, and cotton filling and backing.

Finished size:
59 x 59 inches

1997

This commissioned piece resulted from a design competition for the Dedication Center of the Williamsburg Cemetery, Kitchener, Ontario, Canada.

Small Craft Warning

*"**Small Craft Warning** features an exploded paisley print, intended to suggest a magic flying carpet; surely an unsuitable craft in which to navigate the stormy sea that is in the background."*

Ellen Adams

Made using cotton and silk fabrics, glass-seed beads, cotton embroidery floss, and cotton filling and backing.

Finished size:
41 x 41 inches

1998

Taking Stock

"…juxtaposes the image of a fish seen through a large mesh net, with a representation of a running pixel board displaying stock-trading information. The sequins used as pixels are meant to suggest fish scales, far removed from their natural function, and adding to the contrast between the glittery urbane border, and the chaotic, lively underwater scene. This piece is my comment on the depletion of fish stocks on both of our coasts, and [the] extent to which business considerations govern our decisions about stewardship of our natural resources."

Ellen Adams

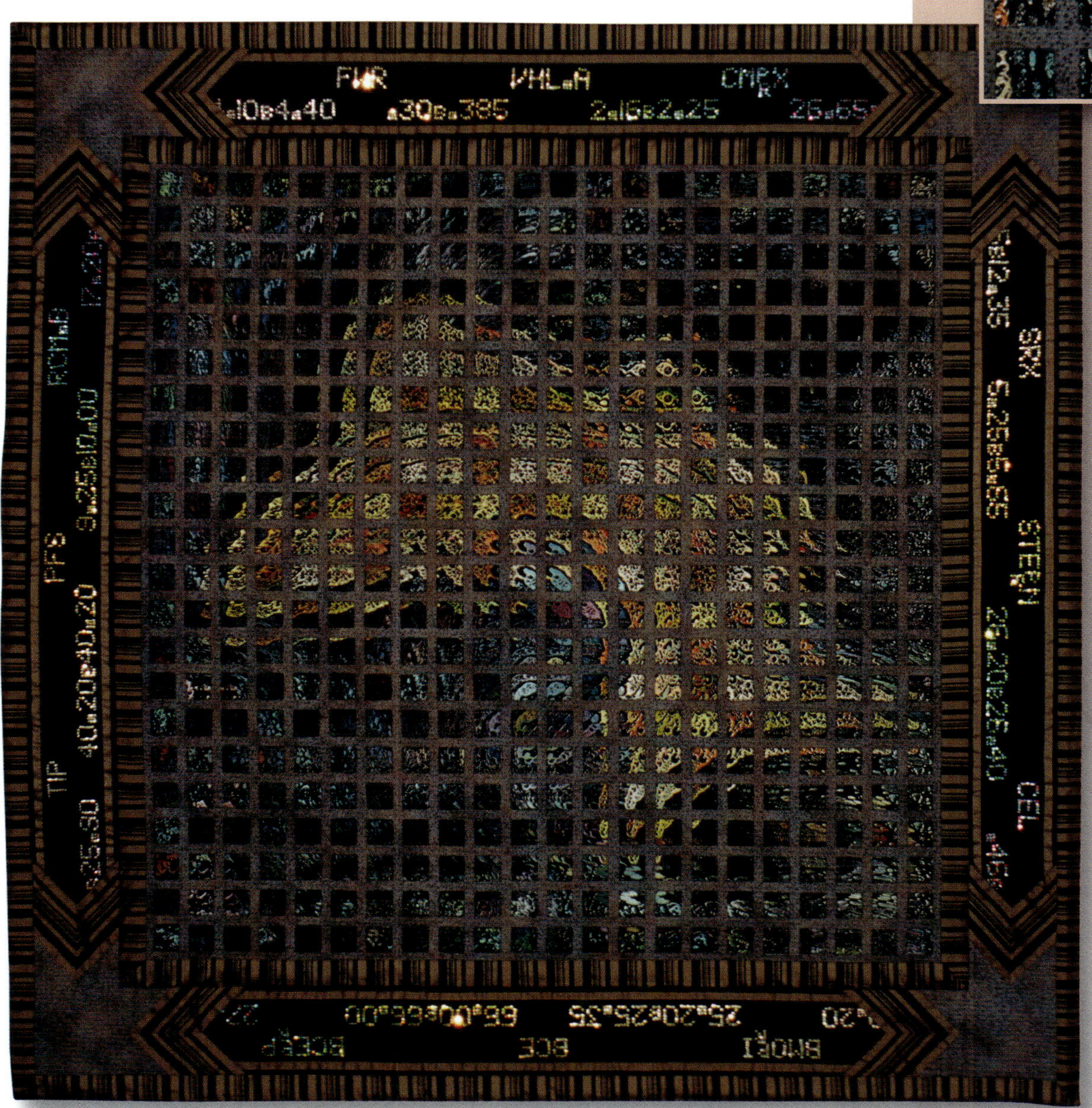

Made using cotton and synthetic fabrics, sequins, seed beads, and cotton filling and backing.

Finished size: 74 x 74 inches

1998

Ellen printed the fabric repeats of a fish motif in black on white fabric, then tinted different copies with various colors. This piece was purchased by the Ontario Municipal Employees Retirement System in Toronto, Canada.

Kathmandu, Nepal

Made using natural and synthetic fabrics, photo transfers, glass-seed beads, cotton embroidery floss, polyester ribbon, and cotton filling and backing.

Finished size:
64 x 42½ inches

1998

"*Kathmandu, Nepal* explores the sense of place by presenting four versions of an old courtyard in Kathmandu. A photograph of a place visited is faithful and objective; one's memory of it may be imperfect, but it is enriched by emotion. The four versions here present increasingly fragmented, though still highly organized views, and suggest moods of neutrality, delight, mystery and foreboding."

Ellen Adams

Occasional Pieces

This was Ellen's last Shattered Image piece.

2000

Project Worksheets

Copy and use these worksheets if you want to practice cutting and arranging a 4, 9, or 16-repeat. This way, you can gain confidence with the technique first and save your fabric for later.

Which Shattered Image technique are you doing?

- 4-repeat
  Make 4 copies of the worksheet on page 83
  (8 x 10 inches).

- 9-repeat
  Make 9 copies of the worksheet on page 84
  (6 x 9 inches).

- 16-repeat
  Make 16 copies of the worksheet on page 83
  (8 x 10 inches).

Shattered Note

Remove Before Copying

For the best results, carefully remove the worksheet page from the book before copying or download them from http://www.shatterandsew.com/worksheets

Use this worksheet for the 9-repeat.

Use the worksheet on page 83 for the 4-repeat and 16-repeat.

Anchor squares — The squares cut from the first image repeat that are labeled A. These squares are the foundation from which you expand the image.

Column placement — Squares arranged vertically.

Grid — Any fabric or diagram with boxes that indicate where you place the squares to create the Shattered Image pattern.

Image — The original motif or focal point of your picture, such as an animal, a flower, or a geometric design.

Image repeat — One occurrence or repeat of your motif or focal point on the fabric.

Motif — A single repeated design or theme.

Offset squares — Squares cut from all other image repeats. Also called B, C, D, and so on.

Row placement — Squares arranged horizontally.

Shattered Image technique — A fast and easy way to cut each repeat *separately* into squares and then arrange each square on a grid, so that floral images appear to bloom, images of animals or vehicles seem to move, and shapes diffuse to abstraction. The minimum number of image repeats used is 4. The maximum can be any number – this book identifies only the following versions:

4-repeat – the simplest form of cutting 4 image repeats into squares and reassembling those squares.

9-repeat – a more complex form of cutting 9 image repeats into squares and reassembling those squares.

16-repeat – the most complex form identified in this book of cutting 16 image repeats into squares and reassembling those squares.

Template — The plastic guide you use to cut image repeats from your fabric.

Sizing — A resinous solution typically used to add stiffness to, or prevent stretching of, synthetic fibers, such as polyester; starch is typically used to add body to non-synthetic fibers such as cotton.

Index

Of the many domestic-engineering skills my mother taught me, sewing and crafts appealed the most.

I enjoyed making clothes or creative projects for the house, but once I entered the work force, my career replaced the need to create…or so I thought! One night while shopping for a baby quilt, I saw a quilting store. The gallery of projects that lined the walls was magical. I thought how fun it would be to do a project like one of those I saw…but I had never quilted before. Then I remembered that I had a closet full of sewing scraps and unfinished projects. Wouldn't it be great to learn to quilt so I could use up my scraps. How many quilters are smiling?

I not only learned to quilt, but I began working at the quilting store one night a week.

When I learned Ellen Adams' Shattered Image technique, I was intrigued to see how images can appear to shimmer, move, or become abstract. I wrote this book in an effort to preserve and share her technique. Ellen was an incredible fiber artist; her gallery of work is shown in Chapter 5 of this book.

I thought about applying this technique to projects that I could make, such as an apron, a wall hanging, or a lap quilt. You'll see them throughout this book. When I began to teach the basics of this technique, I saw the projects my students made and asked them to share their first projects with you. You can see their work in Chapter 3.

I hope you enjoy learning this technique as much as I did and that you'll make many wonderful things incorporating the Shattered Image technique.

Oh yes, and I did make the much-appreciated baby quilt!

Connie Mantini